THE REAL UK DIABETIC AIR FRYER COOKBOOK 2023

The Ultimate Guide to Prepare Healthy Air Fryer Fried Foods with Easy-to-Find Ingredients for a Healthy and Happy Life with Low Fat, Low Sugar, and Low Carbs.

Cathryn J. Goodrich

INTRODUCTION

Diabetes is a condition in which the body's ability to manage the quantity of glucose in the bloodstream is impaired, resulting in a buildup of glucose (also known as sugar) in the blood. Because cells require glucose for fuel, a shortage of insulin or the body's inability to utilise insulin efficiently causes fatty tissue disintegration. This breakdown creates acids known as ketones, which accumulating in the blood and cause ketoacidosis. As ketones accumulate in the body, they transform into stronger acids, further damaging human components.

People with diabetes should consume a low-fat, high-fibre diet to regulate their blood sugar levels. Before making any modifications to your typical regimen, consult with your doctor. Instead of two or three large meals, eating multiple small meals and snacks throughout the day helps maintain steady blood sugar levels. Fitness is also crucial in diabetes control, but you should see your doctor before beginning any exercise regimen.

Diabetes's most common early symptoms are frequent urination and excessive thirst. Maintaining weight is one of the essential methods to prevent diabetes. Eating a nutritious diet and exercising are the greatest ways to reduce your risk of diabetes and maintain your weight. If you are overweight, even decreasing 5 to 10% of your body weight can significantly influence your health. You can do this by eating less and exercising more. A diet high in fibre, low in fat, and low in cholesterol is recommended. You should also exercise for at least 30 minutes most days of the week.

LIVING WITH DIABETES

Many diabetic patients and their families face daily challenges due to their diabetes. The good news is that most diabetics can manage their illnesses, and you can control your diabetes. Maintaining your blood sugar levels within the range suggested by your doctor may be tough. This is because various factors can cause your blood sugar levels to varying, frequently unexpectedly. The factors listed below may have an impact on your blood sugar levels.

FOOD

Whether you have diabetes or not, a nutritious diet is an important part of a healthy lifestyle. If you have diabetes, you must understand how meals affect your blood sugar levels. It is not just what you eat but also how much you eat and how you blend different types of food.

What you should do:

- **Learn about carbohydrate counting and portion sizes.** Many diabetes control options include learning how to count carbohydrates. Carbohydrates have the most impact on blood sugar levels. People who use mealtime insulin must understand the number of carbohydrates in their food to obtain the optimal insulin dose. Examine the appropriate portion size for each meal type. To make meal planning easier, write down the number of items you often consume. Use measuring cups or a scale to make sure proper portion size and an accurate carbohydrate count.
- **Make sure that each meal is well-balanced.** As much as possible, plan your meals to incorporate a range of cereals, fruits and vegetables, proteins, and fats. Take note of the carbohydrates you ingest. Some carbohydrates, such as fruits, vegetables, &whole grains, are better for you than others. These meals are low in carbohydrates and high in fibre, which helps keep blood sugar levels stable. Consult your doctor, nurse, or nutritionist for the best dietary options and food type balance.
- **Plan your meals and medications.** Concerning your diabetes medications, particularly insulin, eating too little may result in dangerously low blood sugar levels (hypoglycemia). Excessive eating might cause your blood sugar to rise (hyperglycemia). Discuss with your diabetes healthcare team how to manage meal and medication schedules successfully.
- **Drinks with added sugar should be avoided.** Sugary beverages are high in calories and lacking in nutrition. These beverages should be avoided if you have diabetes since they cause blood sugar to surge quickly. The sole exception is if your blood sugar level is low. Sugar-sweetened beverages, such as soda, juice, & sports drinks, can be used to quickly increase low blood sugar levels.

EXERCISE

Physical activity is another important component of your diabetes management plan. While you exercise, your muscles need sugar (glucose) for energy. Regular physical activity also improves your body's insulin utilisation.

These components act together to lower your blood sugar levels. The more intense your workout, the longer the impact lasts. On the other hand, simple jobs like cleaning, gardening, or standing for lengthy periods of time may help your blood sugar.

What you should do:

- **Consult your doctor before beginning an exercise regimen.** Consult your doctor to determine the best type of exercise for you. Most people should engage in at least 150 minutes of moderate aerobic activity weekly. Aim for 30 mins of moderate aerobic activity on most days of the week. If you have been inactive for an extended time, your doctor may want to evaluate your overall health before making a suggestion. He or she may counsel you on the ideal combination of aerobic and muscle-strengthening exercises.
- **Maintain a consistent training schedule.** Consult your doctor about the best time of day to exercise so that your workout routine aligns with your diet and medication regimen.
- **Know your numbers.** Before exercising, talk to your doctor about what blood sugar levels are best for you.
- **Check your blood sugar levels.** Check blood sugar levels before, during, and after exercise, especially if you use insulin or other blood sugar-lowering medications. Exercise can lower blood sugar levels for up to a day after you perform it for the first time or at a higher intensity. Be aware of low blood sugar symptoms, including shakiness, weakness, weariness, hunger, lightheadedness, irritability, anxiety, or disorientation. If you use insulin and your body's blood sugar level is less than 90 mg/dL or 5.0 mmol/L, have a little snack before you begin exercising to avoid hypoglycemia.
- **Stay hydrated.** Drink plenty of water or other fluids when exercising since dehydration might cause blood sugar levels to drop.

- **Make yourself ready.** When exercising, keep a small snack or glucose tablet on hand in case your blood sugar drops too low. Always wear a medical identity bracelet, and adjust your diabetic treatment plan as needed. If you take insulin, you should reduce your insulin dose before exercising and monitor your blood sugar for many hours after severe activity since delayed hypoglycemia can occur. Your doctor may advise you on the best way to modify your medications. If you've upped your exercise routine, you may need to change your treatment.

MEDICATION

When diet and exercise are insufficient to control blood sugar levels, insulin and other diabetic medications are required. However, the efficacy of these medications relies on the dose's timing and magnitude. Medications that treat conditions other than diabetes may affect your blood sugar levels.

What you should do:

- **Insulin must be properly kept.** Insulin improperly stored or past its expiration date may no longer be effective. Insulin is extremely sensitive to temperature changes.
- **Inform your doctor of any problems.** If your diabetic medications consistently cause your blood sugar to drop too low or increase too high, the dosage or timing may need to be adjusted.
- **Be cautious with new medications.** If you are considering taking an OTC drug or if your doctor prescribes a new prescription to treat another ailment, such as high blood pressure or high cholesterol, ask your doctor or pharmacist if the medication may affect your blood sugar levels.
- **In some circumstances, a different medication may be administered.** Before beginning any new over-the-counter medication, see your doctor to ensure you understand how it may affect your blood sugar level.

ILLNESS

When you're sick, your body produces stress chemicals that help you fight the illness but can also raise your blood sugar level. Changes in your appetite and everyday activities might also affect diabetes management.

What you should do:

- **Develop a plan. Make a sick-day plan with your healthcare team.** Include instructions on which medications to take, how often to monitor your blood sugar and urine ketone percentage, how to regulate your medication dosages, and when to notify your doctor.
- **As normal, take your diabetes medicine.** If unable to eat due to nausea or vomiting, contact your doctor. You may need to adjust ur insulin dose or temporarily reduce or eliminate short-acting insulin or diabetic medicine due to the risk of hypoglycemia. However, do not stop taking your long-acting insulin. During illness, it is vital to test your blood glucose often, and your doctor may also advise you to check your urine for the presence of ketones.
- **Maintain your diabetes diet.** Eating regularly will help you control your blood sugar levels if you can. Stock up on stomach-friendly foods like gelatin, crackers, soups, and applesauce. Drink plenty of water or other non-calorie-containing beverages, such as tea, to stay hydrated. If you take insulin, you might need to drink sugary drinks like juice or sports drinks to keep your blood sugar from dropping too low.

ALCOHOL

The liver usually releases stored sugar to adjust for falling blood sugar levels. However, if your liver is too busy metabolising alcohol, your blood sugar level may not get the essential boost. Alcohol can produce low blood sugar levels fast and for up to 24 hours following intake.

What you should do:

- **Obtain your doctor's approval before consuming alcohol.** Alcohol may aggravate diabetes complications such as nerve damage and eye degeneration. However, if your diabetes is under control and your doctor permits, having an alcoholic beverage on occasion is OK. One drink per day for women of any age and men over 65, and two drinks per day for males under 65, is considered moderate alcohol use. One drink equals a 12 ounce beer, 5 ounces of wine, or 1.5 ounces of distilled liquor.
- **Never drink alcoholic beverages on an empty stomach.** If you take insulin or other diabetic medications, eat before drinking or drink with a meal to avoid low blood sugar.

- **Choose your beverages with care.** Light beer and dry wines have less calories and carbohydrates than other types of alcoholic beverages. Sugar-free mixers like diet soda, diet tonic, club soda, or seltzer will not raise your blood sugar levels.
- **Calories should be counted**. Your daily calorie total includes the calories from any alcohol you eat. Inquire with your doctor or a nutritionist about including alcoholic beverage calories and carbohydrates in your diet plan.
- **Check your blood sugar level before going to bed.** Check your blood sugar before bed since alcohol can cause blood sugar levels to decline long after your last drink. If your blood sugar isn't between 100 - 140 mg/dL (5.6 and 7.8 mmol/L), eat something before night to compensate for the drop.

HEALTHY EATING TIPS FOR DIABETES

1. Daily basis, eat three meals, including breakfast.
2. Make an effort to avoid skipping meals.
3. Meals should be spaced out by 4 to 6 hours.
4. Breakfast, lunch, and supper portions should be around the same size.
5. Avoid eating overly huge or extremely small portions.
6. Consume one piece of fresh fruit with each meal.
7. Daily, limit yourself to 1/2 cup of juice.
8. Limit your intake of high-fat foods, such as deep-fried or fried foods.
9. Limit meat portions to the size of your hand and eat more fish or skinless chicken.
10. Keep an eye out for unnecessary fats. Dressings and spreads should be low-fat or fat-free.

FOODS AND DRINKS TO LIMITS

Foods and beverages to limit include
- Foods high in saturated fat and trans fat high in sodium sweets, such as baked goods, candy, and ice cream beverages with added sugars, such as juice, regular soda, and typical sports or energy drinks. Instead of sugary drinks, drink water. Use a sugar substitute in your coffee or tea.

Limit your alcohol consumption to one drink per day for ladies and two drinks per day for males. If you take insulin or diabetes drugs that increase the amount of insulin your body generates, alcohol may cause your blood glucose level to drop too low. This is especially true if you haven't eaten in a while. It is advised to have meals when consuming alcohol.

HEALTHY LIVING AND AIR-FRYING

An air fryer is comparable to an oven for roasting and baking. Nonetheless, the heating elements are located on the top and are aided by a powerful, massive fan, resulting in delightfully crisp food in no time. Instead of a vat of hot oil, the air fryer uses spinning heated air to cook food quickly and reliably. This is placed in a metal basket (mesh) or a rack to let hot air flow uniformly over the meal, resulting in the same light golden, crispy crunch as oil frying. It's a straightforward air fryer that cooks food faster than frying and is simple to clean. You may prepare a range of nutritious meals, including fruits, meat, fish, and poultry, as well as healthier versions of your favourite fried foods, such as chips, onion rings, or French fries.

HOW AN AIR FRYER WORKS?

The air fryer is similar to a convection oven but has a hotter tabletop. Its small size allows for speedier cooking. A heating device and a fan are kept at the top of the device. In a basket-style fryer, hot air travels through and around the food. This quick circulation fries the food, similar to deep frying. It's also quite simple to clean, and most systems include dishwasher-safe components.

COOKING WITH AN AIR FRYER

Once you've learned how to use an air fryer, you may use it to reheat frozen foods or cook fresh foods like poultry, salmon, other seafood, pork chops, and vegetables. Because most meats are still wet, they do not require additional oil:
Season to taste with salt and your favourite herbs and spices.
Make sure to use dry spices; less moisture contributes to sharper outcomes.
Baste the steak with any sauce or barbecue sauce in the last few minutes of cooking.
Browning is necessary for lean meat cuts or items with little or no fat, while crisping necessitates the use of an oil spray. Clean and gently oil the pork chops and boneless chicken breasts before cooking. Because of its higher smoke point, vegetable or canola oil is frequently used, guaranteeing that it can survive the high temperatures of an air fryer.
Before being air-fried, vegetables are usually covered with oil. Season with salt and pepper. Use less than you would ordinarily. The crispy air-fried pieces have a lot of flavours. Baby potato halves, broccoli florets, and Brussels sprouts are tasty when fried. They're spotless. Sweet potatoes, butternut squash, peppers, and green beans get sweeter when cooked.

Shake the basket: Before cooking, open the fryer and shake the food around the tray, compressing smaller foods such as French fries and chips. Throw them every 510 minutes to enhance performance.

Avoid overcrowding the basket: Allowing adequate room for meals to allow appropriate air movement is what yields crispy outcomes.

Spray oil on the food: Make sure the food doesn't stick to the bowl. Lightly spray foods with cooking spray.

Make sure the food is thoroughly dry before frying to minimise splattering and excessive smoke (even if you marinate it). Similarly, when making high-fat items like chicken wings, clear the oil from the bottom of the machine regularly.

Other air fryer applications include: The air fryer is perfect for various healthy cooking methods such as grilling, baking, and roasting.

Other tips include:

- Divide the dish into equal parts to ensure uniform cooking.
- Fill the air fryer basket with a single thin, uniform food coating. If the basket is overloaded, the food may get less crispy.
- A modest bit of oil would yield the same light, golden, crispy crust as frying. Using cooking spray or an oil mister, cover the food in a thin, even layer of oil.
- The air fryer is excellent for reheating foods, particularly those with a crispy surface.

BENEFITS OF USING AN AIR FRYER

Reduce your fat and calorie intake.

Let's start with the fundamentals. The built-in high-speed fans of an air fryer evenly distribute air while crisping up food with a thin layer of oil. This gadget makes your meals healthy because it does not require additional oils, allowing you to keep an active lifestyle without compromising your appetite.

With an air fryer, enjoying excellent meals without adding extra calories to your diet is simple. Many studies suggest that cooking using an air fryer decreases the amount of fat by 50 times, resulting in a meal with far fewer calories and fat.

It enables you to keep more nutrients in your diet.

You'll be glad to learn that air fryers can keep nutrients like Vitamin C and polyphenols, commonly lost during traditional cooking methods, intact. They don't simply add a crisp texture and flavour.

Because air fryers utilise less heat than typical ovens, food retains more of its nutritious value and natural taste. This is especially true for antioxidant-rich foods such as fruits and vegetables. Using this culinary tool will add crunch and flavour to your food while preserving the nutritional value of a home-cooked meal.

The usage of an air fryer does not affect your diet.

When it comes to cooking, an air fryer is a great method to save calories and fat. It uses far less oil than typical cooking methods, allowing you to enjoy delicious meals without risking your weight-loss efforts.

Food cooked in an air fryer may help you lose weight by lowering your calorie intake. It only takes a little coating or a few drops of oil to satisfy your cravings while minimising your saturated fat consumption.

Cooking is safer.

One of the advantages of using an air fryer is that it cooks faster and more safely. This equipment consumes less oil and is considerably safer than traditional cooking methods. It implies that you will avoid consuming excess fat, which may raise your risk of heart disease and other health issues.

Furthermore, because air frying takes less time than baking or broiling, you may cook more food in less time. Consequently, it's a wonderful solution for folks who are short on time and can't wait for their food to cook.

Lower Energy Consumption

Air fryers utilise less energy than typical cooking techniques like stovetop or oven cooking and do not require heating or cooling. Furthermore, it produces no toxic smoke or fumes, which is a worry associated with frying on a stovetop or in an oven.

BREAKFAST RECIPE

1. ### CHEESY BELL PEPPER EGGS

Prep Time: 10 minutes
Cook Time: 15 minutes
Servings: 4

Ingredients
- 4 medium green peppers
- 85 g cooked ham, chopped
- 1/4 medium onion, peeled and chopped
- 8 large eggs
- 235 g mild Cheddar cheese

Preparation
1. Remove the tops from all the peppers. With a little knife, cut out the seeds and the white membranes. Each pepper should be filled with ham and onion.
2. Fill each pepper with 2 cracked eggs. Add 59 g of cheese to each pepper. Place in your airfryer basket.
3. Set the timer for 15 minutes and raise the temperature to 198°C.
4. When prepared to perfection, eggs will be hard, and peppers will be soft. Serve right away.

Nutritional information
pre serving calories: 314 protein: 24.9 g fibre: 1.7 g net carbohydrates: 4.5 g fat: 18.5 g sodium: 620 mg Carbohydrates: 6.2 g Sugar: 3.0 g

2. ### LEMON POPPY SEED CAKE

Prep Time: 10 minutes
Cook Time: 14 minutes
Serving: 6

Ingredients
- 96 g blanched finely ground almond flour
- 12 g powdered erythritol
- 2.5 ml bicarbonate of soda
- 57 g unsalted butter, melted
- 60 ml unsweetened almond milk
- 2 large eggs
- 5 ml vanilla extract
- 1 medium lemon
- 5 ml poppy seeds

Preparation
1. Almond flour, bicarbonate of soda, erythritol, butter, almond milk, eggs, & vanilla are combined in a sizable basin.
2. Lemons should be cut in half, the juice squeezed into a small basin, and then added to the batter.
3. Lemon zest should be finely grated; add 15 ml of lemon zest to the mixture and whisk. To the batter, add poppy seeds.
4. Fill a 6" round nonstick cake pan with the batter. In the air fryer basket, put the pan.
5. Set the timer for 14 minutes and raise the temperature to 149°C.
6. A toothpick inserted in the centre will largely come out clean when the food is thoroughly cooked. As it cools, the cake will firm up and finish cooking. At room temperature, serve.

Nutritional information
per serving calories: 204 protein: 6.3 g fibre: 2.4 g net carbohydrates: 2.4 g sugar alcohol: 12.0 g fat: 18.1 g sodium: 72 mg Carbohydrates: 16.8 g Sugar: 0.9 g

3. ### SPAGHETTI SQUASH FRITTERS

Prep Time: 15 minutes
Cook Time: 8 minutes
Serving: 4

Ingredients
- 473 ml cooked spaghetti squash
- 28 g unsalted butter, softened
- 1 large egg
- 60 ml blanched finely ground almond flour
- 2 stalks green onion, sliced
- 2.5 ml garlic powder
- 5 ml dried parsley

Preparation

1. Using a cheesecloth or dish towel, drain the squash of extra moisture.
2. In a sizable bowl, combine each item. Into four patties, form.
3. To fit your air fryer basket, cut a piece of parchment.
4. Each patty should be placed on the parchment before going into the air fryer basket.
5. Set the timer for 8 minutes and raise the temperature to 204°C.
6. Halfway through the cooking process, flip the patties.
7. Serve hot.

Nutritional information
per serving calories: 131 protein: 3.8 g fibre: 2.0 g net carbohydrates: 5.0 g fat: 10.2 g sodium: 32 mg Carbohydrates: 7.0 g Sugar: 2.3 g

4. SAUSAGE AND CHEESE BALLS

Prep Time: 10 minutes
Cook Time: 12 minutes
Servings: 16 balls (4 per serving)

Ingredients
- 454 g pork breakfast sausage
- 60 g shredded Cheddar cheese
- 28 g full-fat cream cheese, softened
- 1 large egg

Preparation
1. In a sizable bowl, combine each item. 16 (1") balls should be formed. Put the balls in the basket of the air fryer.
2. Set the timer for 12 minutes and raise the temperature to 204°C.
3. During cooking, shake the basket two or three times. When fully cooked, sausage balls should be browned on the outside and have internal temp of at least 63°C.
4. Serve hot.

5. BREAKFAST CALZONE

Prep Time: 15 minutes
Cook Time: 15 minutes
Serving: 4

Ingredients
- 337 g shredded mozzarella cheese
- 48 g blanched finely ground almond flour
- 28 g full-fat cream cheese
- 1 large whole egg
- 4 large eggs, scrambled
- 227 g cooked breakfast sausage, crumbled
- 117 g shredded mild Cheddar cheese

Preparation
1. Add cream cheese, mozzarella, and almond flour to a sizable microwave-safe bowl for one minute in a microwave. Stir the ingredients until it becomes uniform and forms a ball. Stir in the egg until dough forms.
2. Roll out the dough to a thickness of 1/4" between two parchment sheets. Create four rectangles out of the dough.
3. In a big bowl, combine scrambled eggs and cooked sausage. Each piece of dough should receive an equal amount of ingredients. Place each piece of dough on the rectangle's lower half. Sprinkle 29 g of Cheddar over each.
4. To enclose the egg and meat mixture, fold the rectangle over. The edges should be thoroughly closed using a pinch, roll, or wet fork.
5. Place the calzones on a piece of parchment that has been cut to fit your air fryer basket. Put parchment in the basket of the air fryer.
6. The timer should be set for 15 minutes with the temperature adjusted to 193°C.
7. About halfway through the cooking process, flip the calzones. Calzones should be golden in colour when finished. Serve right away.

Nutritional information
calories: 560 protein: 34.5 g fibre: 1.5 g net carbohydrates: 4.1 g fat: 41.3 g sodium: 931 mg Carbohydrates: 5.6 g Sugar: 2.1 g

6. VEGGIE FRITTATA

Prep Time: 15 minutes
Cook Time: 12 minutes
Serving: 4

Ingredients
- 6 large eggs
- 60 ml double cream
- 40 g chopped broccoli
- 13 g chopped yellow onion
- 37 g chopped green pepper

Preparation
1. Whisk eggs and double cream in a sizable bowl. Add the pepper, onion, and broccoli.
2. Fill a 6" round oven-safe baking dish with the mixture. The air fryer basket with the baking dish inside.
3. Set the timer for 12 minutes and raise the temperature to 176°C.
4. When the frittata is finished cooking, the eggs should be thoroughly cooked and hard. Serve hot.

Nutritional information
calories: 168 protein: 10.1 g fiber: 0.6 g net carbohydrates: 2.3 g fat: 11.6 g sodium: 115 mg Carbohydrates: 3.2g Sugar: 1.5 g

7. PUMPKIN SPICE MUFFINS

Prep Time: 10 minutes
Cook Time: 15 minutes
Serving: 6

Ingredients
- 48 g blanched finely ground almond flour
- 12 g granular erythritol

- 2.5 g bicarbonate of soda
- 57 g unsalted butter, softened
- 57 g pure pumpkin purée
- 2.5 ml ground cassia
- 1.25 ml ground nutmeg
- 5 ml vanilla extract
- 2 large eggs

Preparation

1. Almond flour, erythritol, bicarbonate of soda ,butter, pumpkin puree, cassia, nutmeg, and vanilla should all be combined in a sizable basin.
2. Add eggs and whisk slowly.
3. Pour the batter evenly into the six silicone muffin liners. If required, place muffin cups into the air fryer basket in batches.
4. Set the timer for 15 minutes and raise the temperature to 149°C.
5. A toothpick inserted in the centre will largely come out clean when the food is thoroughly cooked. Serve hot.

Nutritional information

per serving calories: 205 protein: 6.3 g fibre: 2.3 g net carbohydrates: 3.0 g sugar alcohol: 12.0 g fat: 18.1 g sodium: 65 mg Carbohydrates: 17.4 g Sugar: 1.3 g

8.   BANANA NUT CAKE

Prep Time: 15 minutes
Cook Time: 25 minutes
Serving: 6

Ingredients

- 96 g blanched finely ground almond flour
- 12 g powdered erythritol
- 17 g ground golden Linseeds
- 10 ml bicarbonate of soda
- 2.5 ml ground cassia
- 57 g unsalted butter, melted
- 12.5 ml banana extract
- 5 ml vanilla extract
- 60 ml full-fat sour cream
- 2 large eggs
- 28 g chopped walnuts

Preparation

1. Almond flour, erythritol, Linseeds,bicarbonate of soda and cassia should all be combined in a sizable basin.
2. Add the butter, sour cream, vanilla, and banana extracts.

3. Gently whisk the eggs into the mixture until everything is incorporated. Add the walnuts and stir.
4. Place in the air fryer basket after pouring onto a 6" nonstick cake pan.
5. Set the timer for 25 minutes and raise the temperature to 149°C.
6. When fully cooked, the cake will be golden, and a toothpick inserted in the centre should come out clean. To prevent crumbling, let the food completely cool.

Nutritional information

per serving calories: 263 protein: 7.6 g fibre: 3.2 g net carbohydrates: 3.1 g sugar alcohol: 12.0 g fat: 23.5 g sodium: 191 mg Carbohydrates: 18.2 g Sugar: 1.3 g

9.   PANCAKE CAKE

Prep Time: 10 minutes
Cook Time: 7 minutes
Serving: 4

Ingredients

- 71 g blanched finely ground almond flour
- 6 g powdered erythritol
- 2.5 ml bicarbonate of soda
- 28 g unsalted butter, softened
- 1 large egg
- 2.5 ml unflavored gelatin
- 2.5 ml vanilla extract
- 2.5 ml ground cassia

Preparation

1. Almond flour, erythritol, and bicarbonate of soda should be combined in a sizable bowl. Add butter, gelatin, cassia, vanilla, and egg. Add to a 6" round baking pan.
2. In the air fryer basket, put the pan.
3. The timer should be set for 7 minutes with the temperature adjusted to 149°C.
4. A toothpick will come out smoothly when the cake is fully baked. Serve cake divided into four pieces.

Nutritional information

per serving calories: 153 protein: 5.4 g fibre: 1.6 g net carbohydrates: 1.9 g sugar alcohol: 9.0 g fat: 13.2 g sodium: 80 mg Carbohydrates: 12.5 g Sugar: 0.5 g

10. BACON, EGG, AND CHEESE ROLL-UPS

Prep Time: 15 minutes
Cook Time: 15 minutes
Serving: 4

Ingredients

- 28 g unsalted butter
- 13 g chopped onion
- 6 large eggs
- 1/2 medium green pepper, seeded and chopped
- 12 slices sugar-free bacon
- 235 g shredded sharp Cheddar cheese
- 120 g mild salsa for dipping

Preparation

1. Melt butter in a medium skillet over medium heat. Add onion & pepper to the skillet then cook for about 3 mins or until the onions are translucent and fragrant.
2. After whisking the eggs, add them to the skillet. For about five minutes, scramble eggs with peppers and onions until they are fully cooked and fluffy. Heat has been removed; set aside.
3. Three bacon slices should be placed side by side, with a slight overlap of 1/4, on a work surface. On the side nearest to you, pile 60 ml scrambled eggs high and top with 56 g of cheese.
4. Roll the bacon tightly around the eggs, and if necessary, tack the seam shut with a toothpick. Put a roll in each of the air fryer's baskets.
5. Set the timer for 15 minutes and raise the temperature to 176°C. Halfway through the cooking process, rotate the rolls.
6. When fully cooked, bacon will be crisp and browned. Serve instantly with salsa on the side for dipping.

Nutritional information

per serving calories: 460 protein: 28.2 g fibre: 0.8 g net carbohydrates: 5.3 g fat: 31.6 g sodium: 1,100 mg Carbohydrates: 6.0 g Sugar: 3.1 g

11. CHEESY CAULIFLOWER HASH BROWNS

Prep Time: 20 minutes
Cook Time: 12 minutes
Serving: 4

Ingredients

- 1 (340 g) steamer bag of cauliflower
- 1 large egg
- 235 g shredded sharp Cheddar cheese

Preparation

1. Cook the contents of the bag in the microwave as directed on the packaging. Let the cauliflower cool completely before putting it in a cheesecloth or dish towel and wringing off the extra liquid.
2. With a fork, mash the cauliflower and mix in the cheese and egg.
3. To fit the air fryer basket, cut a piece of parchment. Shape a quarter of the ingredients into a hash brown patty. Working in batches, if required, place it onto the paper and into the air fryer basket.
4. Set the timer for 12 minutes and raise the temperature to 204°C.
5. About halfway through the cooking process, flip the hash browns. They will be golden brown when fully cooked. Serve right away.

Nutritional information

per serving calories: 153 protein: 10.0 g fibre: 1.7 g net carbohydrates: 3.0 g fat: 9.4 g sodium: 224 mg Carbohydrates: 4.6 g Sugar: 1.8 g

12. SCRAMBLED EGGS

Prep Time: 5 minutes
Cook Time: 15 minutes
Serving: 2

Ingredients

- 4 large eggs
- 28 g unsalted butter, melted
- 60 g shredded sharp Cheddar cheese

Preparation

1. Whisk eggs after cracking them into a 2-cup round baking dish. Put the dish in the basket of the air fryer.
2. Set the timer for 10 minutes and raise the temperature to 204°C.
3. Stir the eggs and include the butter and cheese after five minutes. Stir once again after 3 more minutes of cooking.
4. Give the eggs two more minutes to finish cooking before removing them if they are done to your preference.
5. Fork it up to fluff. Serve hot.

Nutritional information

per serving calories: 358 protein: 19.4 g fiber: 0.0 g net carbohydrates: 1.0 g fat: 27.6 g sodium: 324 mg Carbohydrates: 1.1 g Sugar: 0.5 g

Prep time: 10 minutes
Cooking time: 15 minutes
Servings: 4

Ingredients:

- 1 egg
- 30 ml olive oil
- 45 ml milk
- 99 g plain flour
- 15 ml bicarbonate of soda
- 56 g parmesan, grated
- A splash of Worcestershire sauce

Preparation

1. Stir together the egg, flour, oil, bicarbonate of soda , milk, Worcestershire sauce, and Parmesan in a basin. Divide the mixture among four silicon muffin tins.
2. Place the cups in the cooking basket of your air fryer, cover it, and cook at 200 degrees Celcius for 15 minutes.
3. Breakfast should be served hot.

Nutritional information

per serving: calories 251, fat 6, fibre 8, carbs 9, protein 3

Prep Time: 5 minutes
Cook Time: 12 minutes
 Serving: 4

Ingredients

- 8 slices sugar-free bacon

Preparation

1. Put the air fryer basket with the bacon strips inside.
2. Set the timer for 12 minutes and raise the temperature to 204°C.
3. Flip the bacon after 6 minutes and continue cooking. Serve hot.

Nutritional information

per serving calories: 88 protein: 5.7 g fiber: 0.0 g net carbohydrates: 0.3 g fat: 6.0 g sodium: 357 mg Carbohydrates: 0.2 g Sugar: 0.0 g

Cook Time 6 Minutes
Total Time 6 Minutes
Serving: 4

Ingredients

- 8 raw sausage breakfast patties

Preparation

1. Preheat your air fryer to 187°C.
2. Place the uncooked sausage patties in a single layer in the air fryer, not touching.
3. Cook for 6-8 mins, or until they reach 70°C.
4. Remove from the air fryer and serve immediately!

Nutrition Information:

Calories: 140 total Fat: 10g saturated Fat: 3.5g cholesterol: 35mg Carbohydrates: 0g fiber: 0g sugar: 0g protein: 12g

VEGETARIAN RECIPE

16. AIR FRYER TURNIP FRIES

Prep Time 10 mins
Cook Time 15 mins
Total Time 25 mins
Servings: 4

Ingredients

- 2 medium turnips

Seasoning

- 15 ml avocado oil or olive oil
- 5 ml garlic powder
- 5 ml onion powder
- 5 ml salt

Preparation

1. Peel and cut the turnips into 1/4 inch thick fry.
2. Preheat the air fryer as directed by the manufacturer.
3. In a mixing bowl, combine the oil, salt, and spices.
4. Toss in the turnip fries until evenly coated.
5. Place a single layer of turnip fries in the air fryer basket, spacing them apart so that air can circulate around them.
6. Cook at 200°C for 10-15 minutes or until golden brown. To ensure consistent cooking, shake the basket halfway through.

Nutritional information

Calories: 54kcal Carbohydrates: 5g Protein: 1g Fat: 4g Fiber: 1g

17. SPAGHETTI SQUASH ALFREDO

prep time: 10 minutes
Cook Time: 15 minutes
Serving: 2

Ingredients

- 1/2 large cooked spaghetti squash
- 28 g salted butter, melted
- 120 ml low-carb Alfredo sauce
- 22 g grated vegetarian Parmesan cheese
- 2.5 ml garlic powder
- 5 ml dried parsley
- 1.25 ml ground Black pepper
- 56 g shredded Italian blend cheese

Preparation

1. Take the spaghetti squash strands out of the shell with a fork. Put the food in a big bowl with the Alfredo sauce and butter. Add Black pepper, parsley, garlic powder, and Parmesan to the dish.

2. Place in a 4-cup round baking dish, then sprinkle with cheese shreds. Put the dish in the basket of the air fryer. 3 The timer should be set for 15 minutes with the temperature adjusted to 160°C.
3. The cheese will be browned and bubbling when it is done. Serve right away.

Nutritional information

per serving calories: 375 protein: 13.5 g fibre: 4.0 g net carbohydrates: 20.1 g fat: 24.2 g sodium: 950 mg Carbohydrates: 24.1 g Sugar: 8.0 g

18. BROCCOLI CRUST PIZZA

Prep Time: 15 minutes
Cook Time: 12 minutes
Serves 4

Ingredients

- 340 g riced broccoli, steamed and drained well
- 1 large egg
- 45 g grated vegetarian Parmesan cheese
- 45 ml low-carb Alfredo sauce
- 56 g shredded mozzarella cheese

Preparation

1. Combine broccoli, egg, and ParmesanParmesan in a large mixing basin.
2. Cut parchment paper to fit your air fryer basket. Working in two batches, if required, press out the pizza ingredients to fit on the parchment. Place your air fryer basket in the air fryer.
3. Set the air fryer temperature to 187°C and the timer for 5 minutes.
4. The crust should be solid enough to flip when the timer goes off. If not, add 2 minutes to the time. Turn the crust over.
5. Alfredo sauce and mozzarella cheese on top. Return to the air fryer basket and cook for 7 minutes more or until the cheese is golden and bubbling. Serve hot.

Nutritional information

calories: 136 protein: 9.9 g fibre: 2.3 g net carbohydrates: 3.4 g fat: 7.6 g sodium: 421 mg Carbohydrates: 5.7 g Sugar: 1.1 g

Prep Time: 15 minutes
 Cook Time: 12 minutes
Serving: 2

Ingredients

- 1 (340 g) cauliflower steamer bag
- 1 medium courgette, shredded
- 24 g almond flour
- 1 large egg
- 2.5 ml garlic powder
- 90 g grated vegetarian Parmesan cheese

Preparation

1. Cook the cauliflower as directed on the package, then squeeze out any extra moisture using cheesecloth or paper towels. Put into a large bowl.
2. Put the courgette in the paper towel and blot the excess liquid out. Add to the cauliflower bowl. The rest of the ingredients.
3. Make four patties by evenly dividing the mixture. Create 14"-thick patties by pressing. Each should be placed in the air fryer basket.
4. The timer should be set for 12 minutes with the temperature adjusted to 160°C.
5. When fully cooked, fritters will be firm. Before moving, give it five minutes to cool. Serve hot.

Nutritional information

 per serving calories: 217 protein: 13.7 g fibre: 6.5 g net carbohydrates: 8.5 g fat: 12.0 g sodium: 263 mg
Carbohydrates: 16.1 g Sugar: 6.8 g

Prep Time 3 mins
Cook Time 7 mins
Total Time 10 mins
Servings: 6

Ingredients

- 454 g asparagus
- 15 ml olive oil
- 11 g grated Parmesan
- 5 ml garlic powder
- 5 ml salt
- 1/2 lemon

Preparation

1. Trim the asparagus ends and throw them in a mixing basin.
2. Toss the salad with olive oil to coat.

3. Stir in the ParmesanParmesan, garlic powder, and salt to coat the asparagus.
4. Cook the asparagus in the air fryer basket for 7 minutes at 204 °C, shaking halfway through.
5. Before serving, squeeze lemon over the asparagus.

Nutritional information

Pre serving Calories: 72kcal Carbohydrates: 7g Protein: 4g Fat: 4g | Saturated Fat: 1g Cholesterol: 2mg Fiber: 3g Sugar: 2g

Prep Time: 5 minutes
Cook Time: 15 minutes
Serving 2

Ingredients

- 2 medium green peppers
- 3 large eggs
- 60 ml full-fat ricotta cheese
- 13 g diced yellow onion
- 45 g chopped broccoli
- 117 g shredded medium Cheddar cheese

Preparation

1. Remove the peppers' tops, then use a tiny knife to scrape off the seeds and white membranes.
2. Combine the ricotta and eggs in a medium bowl.
3. Include broccoli and onion. Into each pepper, evenly distribute the egg and veggie mixture. Put Cheddar on top. Fill a 4-cup round baking dish with peppers, then put the baking dish into the air fryer basket.
4. Set the timer for 15 minutes and raise the temperature to 176°C.
5. When thoroughly cooked, eggs will be mainly firm, and peppers will be soft. Serve right away.

Nutritional information

per serving calories: 314 protein: 21.6 g fibre: 3.0 g net carbohydrates: 7.8 g fat: 18.7 g sodium: 325 mg
Carbohydrates: 10.8 g Sugar: 4.5 g

Prep Time: 5 minutes
Cook Time: 12 minutes
Servings 4

Ingredients

- 1 medium aubergine, cut into 1/4" slices
- 2 large tomatoes, cut into 1/4" slices
- 113 g fresh mozzarella, cut into 1/2-ounce slices
- 30 ml olive oil
- 5 g fresh basil, sliced

Preparation

1. Place four slices of aubergine on the bottom of a 6" round baking dish. Each round of aubergine should have a piece of tomato, then some mozzarella, and finally some aubergine. Repetition is required.
2. Add a drizzle of olive oil. Place the dish in the air fryer basket after covering it with foil.
3. Set the timer for 12 minutes and raise the temperature to 176°C.
4. The aubergine will be soft when finished. To serve, garnish with fresh basil.

Nutritional information

per serving calories: 195 protein: 8.5 g fibre: 5.2 g net carbohydrates: 7.5 g fat: 12.7 g sodium: 184 mg Carbohydrates: 12.7 g Sugar: 7.5 g

23.   ROASTED BROCCOLI SALAD BROCCOLI

Prep Time: 10 minutes
Cook Time: 7 minutes
Servings 2

Ingredients

- 213 g fresh broccoli florets
- 28 g salted butter, melted
- 23 g sliced almonds
- 1/2 medium lemon

preparation

1. Place broccoli into a 6" round baking dish. Pour butter over broccoli. Add almonds and toss. Place the dish into the air fryer basket.
2. Adjust the temperature to 193°C and set the timer for 7 minutes.
3. Stir halfway through the cooking time.
4. When the timer beeps, zest the lemon onto the broccoli and squeeze the juice into a pan. Toss. Serve warm.

Nutritional information

per serving calories: 215 protein: 6.4 g fibre: 5.0 g net carbohydrates: 7.1 g fat: 16.3 g sodium: 136 mg Carbohydrates: 12.1 g Sugar: 3.0 g

24.   AIR FRYER GREEN BEANS

Prep Time 2 mins
Cook Time 8 mins
Total Time 10 mins
Servings: 4

Ingredients

- 454 g fresh green beans trimmed
- 15 ml olive oil

- 11 g grated Parmesan cheese
- 5 ml garlic powder
- 5 ml salt
- 1 lemon juice

Preparation

1. Drizzle olive oil over the green beans in a bowl. Toss with the ParmesanParmesan, garlic powder, and salt to mix.
2. Arrange green beans in your air fryer basket and cook at 193°C for 8-10 minutes or until soft.
3. Before serving, squeeze a lemon over the green beans and season with salt to taste.

Nutritional information

per serving Calories: 80kcal Carbohydrates: 9g Protein: 3g Fat: 4g Saturated Fat: 1g Cholesterol: 2mg Fiber: 3g Sugar: 4g

25.   CHEESY CAULIFLOWER PIZZA CRUST

Prep Time: 15 minutes
Cook Time: 11 minutes
Serving 2

Ingredients

- 1 (340 g) steamer bag of cauliflower
- 60 g shredded sharp Cheddar cheese
- 1 large egg
- 14 g blanched finely ground almond flour
- 5 ml Italian blend seasoning

Preparation

1. Cauliflower should be prepared as directed on the package. Remove from the bag and squeeze excess water out using cheesecloth or paper towels. Fill a big basin with cauliflower.
2. In the bowl, combine the cheese, egg, almond flour, and Italian spice.
3. To fit your air fryer basket, cut a piece of parchment. Shape a 6" diameter circle out of cauliflower. Place in the air fryer basket.
4. Set the thermostat to 182 degrees Celsius it and start the timer for 11 minutes.
5. Flip the pizza crust after 7 minutes.
6. Pizza can be topped with your choices. Reposition and cook for a further 4 minutes, or until completely cooked and golden, in the air fryer basket. Serve right away.

Nutritional information

per serving calories: 230 protein: 14.9 g fibre: 4.7 g net carbohydrates: 5.3 g fat: 14.2 g sodium: 257 mg Carbohydrates: 10.0 g Sugar: 4.2 g

Prep Time: 5 minutes
Cook Time: 15 minutes
Serving: 4

Ingredients
- 1 medium head cauliflower
- 28 g salted butter, melted
- 1 medium lemon
- 2.5 ml garlic powder
- 5 ml dried parsley

Preparation
1. Cauliflower should have its leaves removed before being brushed with melted butter. Zest one half of the lemon onto the cauliflower after cutting it in half. Pour the zested lemon half's juice over the cauliflower after you've squeezed it.
2. Add some parsley and garlic powder. Put the head of the cauliflower in the air fryer basket.
3. Set the timer for 15 minutes and raise the temperature to 176°C.
4. Avoid overcooking cauliflower by checking it every 5 minutes. It ought to be knife-tender.
5. Pour lemon juice from the remaining half over the cauliflower before serving. Serve right away.

Nutritional information
per serving calories: 91 protein: 3.0 g fibre: 3.2 g net carbohydrates: 5.2 g fat: 5.7 g sodium: 90 mg Carbohydrates: 8.4 g Sugar: 3.1 g

Prep Time: 15 minutes
Cook Time: 20 minutes
Serving: 2

Ingredients
- 1 large Aubergine
- 28 g unsalted butter
- 1/4 medium yellow onion, diced
- 60 g chopped artichoke hearts
- 1 cup fresh spinach
- 18 g diced red pepper
- 125 g crumbled feta

Preparation
1. Slice the Aubergine in half lengthwise, scoop out the meat, and then reassemble the Aubergine in its shell. Take the scooped-out aubergine, chop it, and set it aside.

2. Add butter and onion to a large pan set over medium heat. About 3 to 5 minutes of sautéing should soften the onions. Pepper, spinach, artichokes, and aubergine should all be diced. Cook the peppers and spinach for a further five minutes or until they soften. After taking it off the heat, gently fold in the feta.
3. Fill each Aubergine shell with the filling before placing it in the air fryer basket.
4. The timer should be set for 20 minutes with the temperature adjusted to 160°C.
5. When cooked, the Aubergine will be soft. Serve hot.

Nutritional information
per serving calories: 291 protein: 9.4 g fibre: 10.8 g net carbohydrates: 11.8 g fat: 18.7 g sodium: 374 mg Carbohydrates: 22.6 g Sugar: 12.5 g

Prep Time: 10 minutes
Cook Time: 8 minutes
Serving 4

Ingredients
- 28 g salted butter
- 13 g diced white onion
- 2.5 ml minced garlic
- 120 g cup double cream
- 56 g full-fat cream cheese
- 113 g shredded sharp Cheddar cheese
- 2 medium courgette, spiralized

Preparation
1. Melt butter in a sizable pot over medium heat. Add the onion and cook for 1-3 minutes or until it starts to soften. After adding the garlic and cooking it for 30 seconds, add the cream and cream cheese.
2. Stir in Cheddar after taking the pan off the heat. Put the sauce, courgette, and other ingredients in a 4-cup circular baking dish. Placing the dish in the air fryer basket after covering it with foil.
3. The timer should be set for 8 minutes with the temperature adjusted to 187°C.
4. Remove the foil after 6 minutes and allow the top to brown for the remaining cooking time. Stir, then plate.

Nutritional information
per serving calories: 337 protein: 9.6 g fibre: 1.2 g net carbohydrates: 4.7 g fat: 28.4 g sodium: 298 mg Carbohydrates: 5.9 g Sugar: 4.3 g

Prep Time: 10 minutes
Cook Time: 15 minutes
Serving: 2

Ingredients

- 91 g broccoli florets
- 88 g quartered Brussels sprouts
- 50 g cauliflower florets
- 1/4 medium white onion, peeled and sliced 1/4" thick
- 1/2 big green pepper, seeded and sliced 1/4" thick
- 15 ml coconut oil
- 10 ml chilli powder
- 2.5 ml garlic powder
- 2.5 ml cumin

Preparation

1. Toss all ingredients in a sizable bowl to coat the vegetables completely in oil and seasoning.
2. Vegetables should be placed in the air fryer basket.
3. Set the timer for 15 minutes and raise the temperature to 182°C.
4. While cooking, shake the pan two or three times. Serve hot.

Nutritional information

per serving calories: 121 protein: 4.3 g fibre: 5.2 g net carbohydrates: 7.9 g fat: 7.1 g sodium: 112 mg Carbohydrates: 13.1 g Sugar: 3.8 g

Prep Time: 10 minutes
Cook Time: 5 minutes
Serving 2

Ingredients

- 15 ml coconut oil
- 1/2 medium green pepper, seeded and chopped
- 13 g diced red onion
- 25 g chopped white mushrooms
- 4 flatbread dough tortillas
- 80 g shredded pepper jack cheese
- 1/2 medium avocado, peeled, pitted, and mashed
- 60 ml full-fat sour cream
- 60 ml mild salsa

Preparation

1. Warm up the coconut oil in a moderate skillet over medium heat. In a skillet, combine the pepper, onion, and mushrooms. Sauté for 3 to 5 minutes or until the peppers start to soften.
2. On a work surface, arrange two tortillas and top each with half a slice of cheese. Add the remaining cheese, the sautéed vegetables, and the final two tortillas to the top. Carefully place the quesadillas in the air fryer basket.
3. Set the thermostat to 204°C, and then set a 5-minute timer.
4. Upto halfway through the cooking process, flip the quesadillas. Serve warm with salsa, avocado, and sour cream.

Nutritional information

per serving calories: 795 protein: 34.5 g fibre: 6.5 g net carbohydrates: 12.9 g fat: 61.3 g sodium: 1,051 mg Carbohydrates: 19.4 g Sugar: 7.4 g

APPETIZER AND SIDES RECIPE

31. ROASTED GARLIC

Prep time 5 minutes
Cook Time: 20 minutes
Serving: 12 cloves (1 per serving)

Ingredients
- 1 medium head garlic
- 10 ml avocado oil

Preparation
1. Remove any peel from the garlic but leave the cloves alone. Remove 1/4 of the head of garlic, exposing the clove tips.
2. Drizzle with avocado oil to finish. Enclose the garlic head fully in a tiny sheet of aluminium foil. Fill the air fryer basket halfway with it.
3. Set the air fryer temperature to 204°C and the timer for 20 minutes. Check it after 15 minutes if your garlic head is smaller.
4. When the garlic is done, it should be golden brown and very soft.
5. To serve, the cloves should readily pop out and be distributed or sliced. Refrigerate in an airtight container for about 5 days. Individual cloves can also be frozen on a baking sheet and then stored together in a freezer-safe storage bag once frozen.

Nutritional information
Per Serving Calories: 11 Protein: 0.3 g Fiber: 0.1 g Net Carbohydrates: 0.8 g Fat: 0.8 g Sodium: 0 mg Carbohydrates: 1.1 g Sugar: 0.0 g

32. PROSCIUTTO-WRAPPED PARMESAN ASPARAGUS

Prep Time: 10 minutes
Cook Time: 10 minutes
Serving: 4

Ingredients
- 454 g asparagus
- 12 (14 g) slices prosciutto
- 15 ml coconut oil, melted
- 10 ml lemon juice
- 0.6 ml red pepper flakes
- 30 g grated Parmesan cheese
- 28 g salted butter, melted

Preparation
1. Place a slice of prosciutto and an asparagus spear on a spotless work surface.
2. Lemon juice and coconut oil should be drizzled on. Over the asparagus, smear Parmesan and red pepper flakes. Wrap the spear of asparagus in prosciutto. Place in your air fryer basket.
3. Set the timer for 10 minutes and raise the temperature to 190°C.
4. Before serving, drizzle some butter over the asparagus roll.

Nutritional information
per serving calories: 263 protein: 13.9 g fibre: 2.4 g net carbohydrates: 4.2 g fat: 20.1 g sodium: 367 mg Carbohydrates: 6.7 g Sugar: 2.1 g

33. GARLIC PARMESAN CHICKEN WINGS

Prep Time: 5 minutes
Cook Time: 25 minutes
Serving: 4

Ingredients
- 907 g raw chicken wings
- 5 ml salt
- 2.5 ml garlic powder
- 15 ml bicarbonate of soda
- 57 g unsalted butter, melted
- 30 g grated Parmesan cheese
- 1.25 ml dried parsley

Preparation
1. Chicken wings, salt, bicarbonate of soda, and 2.5 ml of garlic powder should all be combined in a sizable basin. Put wings in the basket of the air fryer.
2. Set the timer for 25 minutes and raise the temperature to 204°C.
3. During the cooking process, turn the basket two or three times.
4. Combine butter, ParmesanParmesan, and parsley in a small bowl.
5. Place the wings in a clean, big bowl after removing them from the fryer. The butter mixture should be poured over the wings and tossed to coat. Serve hot.

Nutritional information
per serving calories: 564 protein: 41.6 g fiber: 0.1 g net carbohydrates: 2.1 g fat: 42.2 g sodium: 1,067 mg Carbohydrates: 2.1 g Sugar: 0.0 g

34. MOZZARELLA-STUFFED MEATBALL

Prep Time: 15 minutes
Cook Time: 15 minutes
Serving: 16 meatballs (4 per serving)

Ingredients

- 454 g 80/20 ground beef
- 24 g blanched finely ground almond flour
- 5 ml dried parsley
- 2.5 ml garlic powder
- 1.25 ml onion powder
- 1 large egg
- 85 g low-moisture, whole-milk mozzarella, cubed
- 120 ml low-carb, no-sugar-added pasta sauce
- 22 g grated Parmesan cheese

Preparation

1. Combine ground beef, parsley,
2. almond flour, garlic powder, onion powder, and egg in a sizable bowl. Mix ingredients thoroughly by folding them in.
3. Make meatballs out of the mixture that is 2" in diameter, and then press your thumb or a spoon into the middle of each meatball. Form the ball around a cheese cube and place it in the centre.
4. If necessary, add the meatballs to the air fryer in batches.
5. Set the timer for 15 minutes and raise the temperature to 176°C.
6. Meatballs are properly cooked when the internal temperature reaches at least 82°C and the exterior is somewhat crispy.
7. When the meatballs are done cooking, place them in the sauce and top them with grated ParmesanParmesan before serving.

Nutritional information

per serving calories: 447 protein: 29.6 g fibre: 1.8 g net carbohydrates: 3.5 g fat: 29.5 g sodium: 508 mg Carbohydrates: 5.4 g Sugar: 1.5 g

35. GARLIC CHEESE BREAD

Prep Time: 10 minutes
Cook Time: 10 minutes
Serving: 2

Ingredients

- 112 g shredded mozzarella cheese
- 22 g grated Parmesan cheese
- 1 large egg
- 2.5 ml garlic powder

Preparation

1. In a sizable bowl, combine each item. To fit your air fryer basket, cut a piece of parchment. Place the mixture in the air fryer basket after shaping it into a circle on the parchment.
2. Set the timer for 10 minutes and raise the temperature to 176°C.
3. Serve hot.

Nutritional information

per serving calories: 257 protein: 19.1 g fiber: 0.1 g net carbohydrates: 3.7 g fat: 16.6 g sodium: 611 mg Carbohydrates: 3.7 g Sugar: 0.7 g

36. SPICY SPINACH ARTICHOKE DIP

Prep Time: 10 minutes
Cook Time: 10 minutes
Serving: 6

Ingredients

- 283 g frozen spinach, drained and thawed
- 1 (396 g) can of artichoke hearts, drained and chopped
- 60 g chopped pickled jalapeños
- 227 g cream cheese, softened
- 60 ml mayonnaise
- 60 ml sour cream
- 2.5 ml garlic powder
- 22 g grated Parmesan cheese
- 118 g shredded pepper jack cheese

Preparation

1. In a 4-cup baking bowl, combine all the ingredients. Place in your air fryer basket.
2. The timer should be set for 10 mins with the temperature adjusted to 160°C.
3. Remove when bubbling and brown. Serve hot.

Nutritional information

per serving calories: 226 protein: 10.0 g fibre: 3.6 g net carbohydrates: 6.4 g fat: 15.8 g sodium: 775 mg Carbohydrates: 10.1 g Sugar: 3.3

37. BACON-WRAPPED ONION RINGS

Prep Time: 5 minutes
Cook Time: 10 minutes
Serving: 4

Ingredients

- 1 large onion, peeled
- 15 ml sriracha
- 8 slices sugar-free bacon
- 1 Slice onion into 1 /4 "-thick slices.

Preparation

1. Slices of onion should be covered in sriracha. Take two onion rings and wrap bacon around them. Repeat with the leftover bacon and onion. Put the object in the air fryer basket.
2. Set the thermostat to 176°C and start the 10-minute timer.
3. To flip the onion rings, use tongs halfway through cooking. Bacon becomes crispy when it is thoroughly cooked. Serve hot.

Nutritional information

per serving calories: 105 protein: 7.5 g fibre: 0.6 g net carbohydrates: 3.6 g fat: 5.8 g sodium: 400 mg Carbohydrates: 4.3 g Sugar: 2.2 g

38. AIR FRYER FROZEN OKRA

Prep Time 0 mins
Cook Time 15 mins
Servings: 3

Ingredients

- 454 g frozen okra
- olive oil spray or 5 ml olive oil
- 2.5 ml garlic
- 2.5 ml black pepper
- 2.5 ml salt
- Red pepper flakes optional, garnish

Preparation

1. Preheat your air fryer to 204 °C
2. Arrange the frozen okra on your air fryer basket in a single layer.
3. Coat the okra with cooking spray.
4. In a small dish, mix the spices and sprinkle over the frozen okra.
5. Shake the basket or softly massage the spices all over with a brush.
6. Shakes the basket after 15 minutes of air cooking.
7. Serve garnished with red pepper flakes!

Nutritional information

Calories: 33kcal Carbohydrates: 7g Protein: 1g Fat: 1g
Saturated Fat: 1g Fiber: 4g Sugar: 1g

39. GARLIC HERB BUTTER ROASTED RADISHES

Prep Time: 10 minutes
Cook Time: 10 minutes
Serving: 4

Ingredients

- 454 g radishes
- 28 g unsalted butter, melted
- 2.5 ml garlic powder
- 2.5 ml dried parsley
- 1.25 ml dried oregano
- 1.25 ml ground black pepper

Preparation

1. Radishes should have their roots removed and be quartered.
2. Put the ingredients and butter in a small bowl. Place the radishes in the air fryer basket after coating them with the herb butter.
3. Set the timer for 10 minutes and raise the temperature to 176°C.
4. Place the radishes in your air fryer basket and cook for the remaining half an hour. Cook the edges until they start to turn brown.
5. Serve hot.

Nutritional information

per serving calories: 63 protein: 0.7 g fibre: 1.3 g net carbohydrates: 1.7 g fat: 5.3 g sodium: 27 mg Carbohydrates: 2.8 g Sugar: 1.4 g

40. CRISPY BRUSSELS SPROUTS

Prep Time: 5 minutes
Cook Time: 10 minutes
Serving: 4

Ingredients

- 454 g Brussels sprouts
- 15 g coconut oil
- 14 g unsalted butter, melted

Preparation

1. Each Brussels sprout should have all loose leaves removed and be cut in half.
2. Place the sprouts in your airfryer basket after coating them with coconut oil.

3. Set the timer for 10 minutes and raise the temperature to 204°C. Depending on how they are starting to brown, you might want to give them a gentle stir midway through the cooking process.
4. They should be soft and have darker caramelized patches when fully cooked. Remove from the frying basket and top with butter that has been melted. Serve right away.

Nutritional information

per serving calories: 90 protein: 2.9 g fibre: 3.1 g net carbohydrates: 4.4 g fat: 6.0 g sodium: 20 mg Carbohydrates: 7.4 g Sugar: 1.9 g

41. COURGETTE PARMESAN CHIPS

Prep Time: 10 minutes
Cook Time: 10 minutes
Serving: 4

Ingredients

- 2 medium courgette
- 28 g pork rinds
- 45 g grated Parmesan cheese
- 1 large egg

Preparation

1. Slice a 1/4" thick piece of courgette. Place for 30 minutes to drain excess moisture between two layers of paper towels or a clean kitchen towel.
2. Pork rinds should be placed in a food processor and pulse until very fine. Pour into a large bowl, then stir in the ParmesanParmesan.
3. In a small bowl, beat the egg.
4. Slices of courgette should be well coated after being dipped in egg and then pork rind mixture. Working in batches as necessary, carefully arrange each slice in a single layer into the air fryer basket.
5. Set the timer for 10 minutes and raise the temperature to 160°C. 6 After six minutes of frying, turn the chips over. Serve hot.

Nutritional information

per serving calories: 121 protein: 9.9 g fibre: 0.7 g net carbohydrates: 3.1 g fat: 6.7 g sodium: 363 mg Carbohydrates: 3.8 g Sugar: 1.6 g

42. KALE CHIPS

Prep Time: 5 minutes
Cook Time: 5 minutes
Serving: 4

Ingredients

- 4 cups stemmed kale
- 10 ml avocado oil
- 2.5 ml salt

Preparation

1. Kale should be mixed with avocado oil and salt in a big dish. Place in your air fryer basket.
2. Set the thermostat to 204°C, and then set a 5-minute timer.
3. When cooked, kale will be crunchy. Serve right away.

Nutritional information

per serving calories: 25 protein: 0.6 g fiber: 0.4 g net carbohydrates: 0.7 g fat: 2.1 g sodium: 294 mg Carbohydrates: 1.1 g Sugar: 0.4 g

43. BUFFALO CAULIFLOWER

Prep Time: 5 minutes
Cook Time: 5 minutes
Serving: 4

Ingredients

- 256 g cauliflower florets
- 28 g salted butter, melted
- 1/2 (28 g) dry ranch seasoning packet
- 64 g buffalo sauce

Preparation

1. Cauliflower should be mixed with butter and dry ranch in a big bowl. Place in your air fryer .
2. Set the thermostat to 204°C, and then set a 5-minute timer.
3. During cooking, shake the basket two or three times. When the cauliflower is ready, remove it from the fryer basket and add the buffalo sauce. Serve hot.

Nutritional information

per serving calories: 87 protein: 2.1 g fibre: 2.1 g net carbohydrates: 5.2 g fat: 5.7 g sodium: 802 mg Carbohydrates: 7.1 g Sugar: 2.1 g

Prep Time: 10 minutes
Cook Time: 7 minutes
Serving: 4

Ingredients

- 128 g chopped cauliflower florets
- 30 ml coconut oil, melted
- 10 ml chilli powder
- 2.5 ml garlic powder
- 1 medium lime
- 15 g chopped cilantro

Preparation

1. Cauliflower should be mixed with coconut oil in a big dish. Garlic and chilli powder should be added. Put the air fryer basket with the seasoned cauliflower inside.
2. Set the timer for 7 minutes and raise the temperature to 176°C.
3. The cauliflower will be soft, and its edges will start to become golden. Add to the serving bowl.
4. Squeeze the lime juice over the cauliflower after cutting it into quarters. Cilantro is a good garnish.

Nutritional information

per serving calories: 73 protein: 1.1 g fibre: 1.1 g net carbohydrates: 2.2 g fat: 6.4 g sodium: 15 mg Carbohydrates: 3.3 g Sugar: 1.1 g

Prep time 10 minutes
Cook Time: 5 minutes
Serving: 4

Ingredients

- 473 ml water
- 454 g radishes
- 1.25 ml onion powder
- 1.25 ml paprika
- 2.5 ml garlic powder
- 15 ml coconut oil, melted

Preparation

1. On the stovetop, add water to a medium pot and bring it to a boil.
2. Each radish should have the top and bottom cut off before being thinly and consistently sliced on a mandoline. For this stage, you can alternatively use the food processor's slicing blade.

3. Slices of radish should be boiled for five minutes or until transparent. To remove extra moisture, remove them from the water and place them onto a fresh kitchen towel.
4. Toss the radish chips with the remaining items in a big bowl until they are completely covered with oil and spices. Put the air fryer basket with the radish chips inside.
5. The timer should be set for 5 minutes with the temperature adjusted to 160°C.
6. During the cooking process, shake the basket two or three times. Serve hot.

Nutritional information

per serving calories: 77 protein: 0.8 g fibre: 1.8 g net carbohydrates: 2.1 g fat: 6.4 g sodium: 40.2 mg Carbohydrates: 4.0 g Sugar: 1.9 g

Prep Time: 15 minutes
Cook Time: 5 minutes
Serving: 4

Ingredients

- 2 medium avocados
- 28 g pork rinds, finely ground

Preparation

1. Each avocado is divided in half. Eliminate the pit. Slice the flesh into 14"-thick slices after peeling it with care.
2. In a medium bowl, add the pork rinds and press each avocado slice into the pork rinds to coat them evenly. Put the pieces of avocado in the air fryer basket.
3. Set the timer for 5 minutes and raise the temperature to 176°C.
4. Serve right away.

Nutritional information

per serving calories: 153 protein: 5.4 g fibre: 4.6 g net carbohydrates: 1.3 g fat: 11.7 g sodium: 120 mg Carbohydrates: 5.9 g Sugar: 0.3 g

BEEF RECIPE

47. PEPPERCORN-CRUSTED BEEF TENDERLOIN

Prep Time: 10 minutes
Cook Time: 25 minutes
Serving: 6

Ingredients

- 28 g salted butter, melted
- 10 ml minced roasted garlic
- 45 ml ground 4-Black pepper blend
- 1 (907 g) beef tenderloin, trimmed of visible fat

Preparation

1. Combine the butter and roasted garlic in a small bowl. Over the steak tenderloin, brush it.
2. Roll the tenderloin through the ground Black pepper on a dish to form a crust. The tenderloin should be placed in the air fryer basket.
3. The timer should be set for 25 minutes with the temperature adjusted to 204°C.
4. Halfway through the cooking process, turn the tenderloin.
5. Before slicing, let the meat 10 minutes to rest.

Nutritional information

per serving calories: 289 protein: 34.7 g fiber: 0.9 g net carbohydrates: 1.6 g fat: 13.8 g sodium: 96 mg Carbohydrates: 2.5 g Sugar: 0.0 g

48. CRISPY BEEF AND BROCCOLI STIR-FRY

Prep Time: 1 hour
Cook Time: 20 minutes
Servings: 2

Ingredients

- 227 g sirloin steak, thinly sliced
- 30 ml soy sauce (or liquid aminos)
- 1.25 ml grated ginger
- 1.25 ml finely minced garlic
- 15 ml coconut oil
- 142 g broccoli florets
- 1.25 ml crushed red Pepper
- 0.6 ml xanthan gum
- 2.5 ml sesame seeds

Preparation

1. To marinate the beef, combine it with the soy sauce, ginger, garlic, and coconut oil in a large mixing dish or storage bag. Allow marinating in the refrigerator for 1 hour.
2. Remove the beef from the marinade, retain the marinade, and place it in the air fryer basket.
3. Set the Air fryer temperature to 160°C and the timer for 20 minutes.
4. After 10 minutes, shake the fryer basket with broccoli and red Pepper.
5. Bring the marinade to a boil in a skillet over medium heat, then lower it to a simmer. Allow thickening after adding the xanthan gum.
6. When the air fryer timer goes off, rapidly empty the fryer basket into the skillet and toss. Sesame seeds are optional. Serve right away.

Nutritional information

Calories: 342 Protein: 27.0 g Fiber: 2.7 g Net Carbohydrates: 6.9 g Fat: 18.9 g Sodium: 418 mg Carbohydrates: 9.6 g Sugar: 1.6 g

49. CHORIZO AND BEEF BURGER

Prep Time: 10 minutes
Cook Time: 15 minutes
Servings: 4

Ingredients

- 340 g ground beef
- 113 g ground chorizo
- 13 g chopped onion
- 5 slices pickled jalapeños, chopped
- 10 ml chilli powder
- 5 ml minced garlic
- 1.25 ml cumin

Preparation

1. Combine all of the ingredients in a large mixing basin. Form the mixture into four burger patties by dividing it into four parts.
2. Working in batches, if required, place the burger patties in the air fryer basket.
3. Set the air fryer temperature to 190°C and the timer for 15 minutes.
4. Halfway through the cooking time, flip the patties.
5. Serve hot.

Nutritional information

Per Serving Calories: 291 Protein: 21.6 g Fiber: 0.9 g Net Carbohydrates: 3.8 g Fat: 18.3 G Sodium: 474 mg Carbohydrates: 4.7 g Sugar: 2.5 g

50. CLASSIC MINI MEATLOAF

Prep Time: 10 minutes
Cook Time: 25 minutes
Serving: 6

Ingredients

- 454 g ground beef
- 1/4 medium yellow onion, peeled and diced
- 1/2 medium green pepper, seeded and diced
- 1 large egg
- 21 g blanched finely ground almond flour
- 15 ml Worcestershire sauce
- 2.5 ml garlic powder
- 5 ml dried parsley
- 28 g concentrate
- 60 ml water
- 15 ml powdered erythritol

Preparation

1. Combine ground beef, onion, Pepper, egg, and almond flour in a large mixing basin. Pour in the Worcestershire sauce and season with garlic powder and parsley. Mix until completely mixed.
2. Divide the batter in half and bake in two (4") loaf pans.
3. Combine the concentrate, water, and erythritol in a small basin. Half of the mixture should be spooned over each loaf.
4. Place bread pans into the air fryer basket, working in batches as required.
5. Set the air fryer temperature to 176°C and the timer for 25 minutes, or until the interior temperature reaches 82°C.
6. Serve hot.

Nutritional information

Per Serving Calories: 170 Protein: 14.9 g Fiber: 0.9 g Net Carbohydrates: 2.6 g Sugar Alcohol: 1.5 g Fat: 9.4 g Sodium: 85 mg Carbohydrates: 5.0 g Sugar: 1.5 g

51. PERFECT AIR FRYER RIBEYE STEAK RECIPE

Prep Time 5 minutes
Cook Time 12 minutes
Total Time 17 minutes
Servings: 1-2

Ingredients
Steak
- 1-2 (227 g) Boneless ribeye steak
- Black pepper and salt

Garlic Butter

- 14 g unsalted butter
- 2.5 ml minced garlic
- 1.25 ml fresh thyme

Preparation

1. Preheat your air fryer for 2 mins at 204 °C. Season steaks on both sides with salt & Black pepper.
2. Cook the steak for 12 minutes in the air fryer basket, rotating halfway through. Allow the steak to rest for 8–10 minutes.
3. Meanwhile, mix the butter, garlic, and thyme in a small dish and set aside.
4. Top the meat with garlic butter. Enjoy!

Nutrition Information:

Calories: 170 Fat: 14g Saturated Fat: 7g Cholesterol: 48mg Carbohydrates: 1g Fiber: 0g Sugar: 0g Protein: 11g

52. AIR FRYER MARINATED FLANK STEAK

Prep Time: 5
Refrigerate: 2 hours
Cook Time: 10 minutes
Total Time: 2 hours 15 minutes
Servings: 4

Ingredients

- 227 g flank steak
- 63 ml low sodium soy sauce
- 1/4 Balsamic or Italian dressing
- 5.8 grams brown sugar, regular or sugar substitute
- 10 ml garlic paste or 5 ml ground garlic
- 30 ml Worcestershire sauce
- 30 ml chilli garlic sauce or 2.5 ml red pepper flakes
- 5 ml beef paste or bouillon
- salt and Pepper to taste

Preparation

1. In a dish or zipper-style bag, combine the marinade ingredients. Refrigerate the steak for at least 2 hrs, but not more than 24 hours, in a bag or dish.
2. When ready to cook, let the steak come to room temperature for about 30 minutes before removing it from the marinade.
3. Preheat the air fryer for 5 minutes at 204 °C.
4. Spray nonstick oil spray on the inside surface or grill insert.
5. Cook for 4 minutes on one side of the steak. Cook for another 3 minutes, then test with a meat thermometer. Cook for a further 5 minutes if necessary.

6. Transfer the steak to a dish and set aside for 5-10 minutes to allow the juices to redistribute. To serve, cut against the grain.

Nutritional information

Calories 256 Fat 10.2g Cholesterol 85mg Sodium 1486.8mg Carbohydrate 7.2g Dietary Fiber 0.1g Sugars 4.8g Protein 31.7g

53. AIR FRYER ROAST BEEF

Prep Time 5 Minutes
Cook Time 40 Minutes
Additional Time 30 Minutes
Total Time 1 Hour 15 Minutes
Servings: 4-6

Ingredients
- 907 g roast beef (top roast)
- 15 ml olive oil
- 10 ml salt
- 10 ml pepper

Preparation
1. Remove the beef roast from the refrigerator, then baste it with oil and season with salt and Pepper.
2. Allow the beef roast to come to room temperature for about 30 minutes.
3. Preheat your air fryer to 193 °C.
4. Cook the roast beef in your air fryer for 40-42 mins, turning after about 15 mins.
5. Take out the roast beef from your air fryer when it reaches 1 degree below the required temperature, set aside for at least 10 mins, and serve!

Nutrition Information:

Calories: 195 total Fat: 7g saturated Fat: 2g cholesterol: 77mg sodium: 1995mg carbohydrates: 1g fiber: 0g sugar: 0g protein: 28g

54. AIR FRYER PRIME RIB

Prep Time 5 mins
Cook Time 1 Hrs 15 mins
Rest Time 20 mins
Total Time 1 Hrs 40 mins
Servings: 5-6

Ingredients
- 2721 g Prime Rib
- 45 ml olive oil
- 7.5 ml salt
- 7.5 ml black pepper
- 5 ml smoked paprika
- 5 ml garlic powder
- 34 g minced garlic (about 10 cloves)
- One sprig of fresh rosemary, chopped (or 2.5 ml dried rosemary)
- One sprig of fresh thyme, chopped (or 2.5 ml dried thyme)

Preparation
1. Preheat your air fryer to 198°C.
2. Rub the prime rib generously with olive oil, then season with salt, black Pepper, paprika, and garlic powder.
3. Crush the garlic over the prime rib, then sprinkle with the rosemary and thyme.
4. For the finest flavour, use fresh rosemary and thyme, but dried can still be used.
5. Cook the prime rib gently in the air fryer for 20 minutes.
6. Turn the temperature down to 157 °C and continue to cook for about 55 minutes, or until the Instant-Read Thermometer achieves the desired doneness — 54 °C for medium-rare.
7. Let the prime rib rest for 20 to 30 minutes before slicing and serving.

Nutrition Information:

Calories: 810 Fat: 65g saturated Fat: 25g cholesterol: 188mg sodium: 408mg carbohydrates: 1g fiber: 0g sugar: 0g protein: 51g

55. KETO MEATBALLS WITH ALMOND FLOUR

Prep Time 2 hrs
Cook Time 12 mins
Total Time 2 hrs 12 mins

Ingredients
For the meatballs
- 1 kg (2.2 pounds) ground beef (or half pork, half beef)
- 1 egg
- 2.5 ml salt
- 10 ml freshly ground black Pepper
- 10 ml oregano
- 5 ml basil
- 5 ml thyme
- 2.5 ml chilli flakes
- 1 medium onion (~ 115 grams)
- 6 to 8 crushed garlic cloves
- 15 ml olive oil

For the almond flour panade
- 200 grams of beef stock

- 15 ml unflavored powdered gelatin
- 75 grams of almond flour

Preparation

Almond flour panade

1. (Begin this step early to allow the gelatin to harden) Fill a medium bowl halfway with heated stock and add one spoonful of gelatin. Allow a few minutes for the flower to blossom. With a fork, combine the gelatin. If it isn't totally dissolved, put it in the microwave for a few seconds at a time until it's completely liquid. Do not bring the mixture to a boil.
2. Mix in the almond flour well with the dissolved gelatin.
3. Refrigerate it until it is firm (about 2 hours)
4. Cut the firm gelatin into thin slices with a knife and smash it with a fork until it forms a crumble.

Keto meatballs

1. Chop the onion finely and smash the garlic cloves in a saucepan with one tablespoon of olive oil. Cook over medium heat until transparent, then reduce to low heat and continue to cook until they are a deep golden brown colour. Allow them to cool.
2. Combine your ground meat of choice, 1 egg, 7.5 mL of salt (or to taste), spices, the almond flour panade, and the sauteed onion and garlic.
3. Shape the meatballs using your hands. One batch yields around 24 ping-pong-sized meatballs. Press them lightly, just enough to preserve the form.
4. Preheat the air fryer to 200 degrees Celsius. Spread the meatballs in a single layer in the basket, leaving some space between them for the hot air to circulate.
5. Cook each batch of meatballs for 10 to 12 minutes or until lightly browned and cooked through (add 4-5 minutes if cooking from frozen).

Nutrition Information:

Calories: 330 Total Fat: 17.4g Carbohydrates: 5.1g net Carbohydrates: 3.5g fibre: 1.7g Sugar: 1.6g Protein: 38.4g

56. AIR FRYER CORNED BEEF

Prep Time 10 mins
Cook Time 1 hr 45 mins
Total Time 1 hr 55 mins
Servings: 6-8

Ingredient

- 60 ml brown mustard
- Pickling packet (that comes with your corned beef)
- 15 ml apple cider vinegar
- 1.8 kg corned beef brisket

Preparation

1. Preheat the air fryer to 182 °C.
2. Make a paste using the pickling packet components, mustard, and apple cider vinegar.
3. Place the brisket on a big piece of aluminium foil that has been gently coated with cooking oil. Brush 2/3 of the mustard paste over the entire brisket, saving the remainder, then wrap the beef in foil.
4. Cook the wrapped brisket for 1 hour in the air fryer basket.
5. When the timer goes off, remove the foil and baste the brisket with the leftover sauce before covering it. Cook for another 40 minutes.
6. If you want a lovely top, remove the foil and cook for 5 minutes at 204 degrees C.

Nutrition Information:

Calories: 661 total Fat: 42g saturated Fat: 17g cholesterol: 240mg sodium: 195mg carbohydrates: 0g fiber: 0g sugar: 0g protein: 66g

57. AIR FRYER LONDON BROIL

Prep Time 5 mins
Cook Time 8 mins
Resting Time 10 mins
Total Time 23 mins
Servings: 4

Ingredients

- 680 g top round London Broil
- 5 ml olive oil
- 10 ml Montreal Steak Seasoning

Preparation

1. Preheat your air fryer to 204°C.
2. Rub the meat with oil, then season with Montreal Steak seasoning.
3. Cook the London broil in the air fryer for 8 to 10 mins, depending on the thickness of the steak, or until it achieves the desired doneness (this timing is for medium-rare).
4. Remove the London broil from your air fryer and set aside for 10 minutes before slicing and serving.

Nutrition Information:

Calories: 445 total Fat: 22g saturated Fat: 8g cholesterol: 186mg sodium: 357mg carbohydrates: 1g fiber: 0g sugar: 0g protein: 61g

58. KETO BACON CHEDDAR STUFFED AIR FRYER BURGERS

Prep Time: 15 minutes
Cook Time: 15 minutes
Servings: 4

Ingredients

- 680 g ground beef
- 2.5 ml dried onion
- 1.25 ml garlic powder
- 1.25 ml dry mustard
- 1.25 ml paprika
- 2.5 ml salt
- 1.25 ml pepper
- 60 g cheddar cheese shredded
- 4 slices bacon cooked, chopped

Preparation

1. Preheat your air fryer to 190°C. In a mixing bowl, combine the ground beef and all of the ingredients. Make 142 g balls out of your ground meat.
2. Divide each ball into two parts. Form the bottom patty of your loaded burger with 85 g. In the centre of the bottom patty, make a well. 30 g of cheese should be placed in the centre of the burger. 1 piece cooked, chopped bacon on top to cover the filled burger and flatten the remaining 57 g of ground beef. Glue the edges together. Continue with the remaining burgers.
3. Place the four filled burgers on the air fryer grate. Set an 8-minute timer. Set the timer for 6 mins and flip the burgers. Using an internal thermometer, check the centre of the burgers. The temperature should be 71 °C. If preferred, top burgers with cheese and cook for 1 minute more to melt the cheese.
4. Serve right away. Serve with bacon, pickles, onion, mayo, mustard, and avocado in a lettuce wrap.

Nutritional information

Calories: 513kcal Carbs: 1g Protein: 31g Fat: 42g Sat Fat: 17g Cholesterol: 130mg Fiber: 1g Sugar: 1g

59. AIR FRYER HAMBURGER STUFFED MUSHROOMS

Prep Time: 10 mins
Cook Time: 12 mins
Total Time: 22 mins
Servings: 2

Ingredients

- 2 large portobello mushrooms
- 170 g ground beef
- 1.25 ml salt
- 1.25 ml garlic powder
- 1.25 ml ground black pepper
- 5 ml melted butter
- Hamburger toppings: lettuce, tomato, pickle, cheese, ketchup, mustard, mayo

Preparation

1. Take the stems off the portobello mushrooms.
2. In a mixing bowl, mix the ground beef, salt, garlic powder, and black Pepper. Form two circular patties out of the steak that will fit within your mushrooms.
3. Stuff the mushroom with ground meat.
4. Preheat your air fryer for 3-5 mins at 180° C. Spray the basket lightly with oil. Cook for 6 minutes with the mushrooms in the basket. Open the basket and brush the filled mushrooms with butter on the tops and sides.
5. Cook for another 6 minutes. If you like to melt cheese on top, add a piece with one minute left (any longer, and it might slide off the top).
6. Take the filled mushrooms out of the basket. Garnish with your preferred garnishes.

Nutritional information

Calories: 254kcal Carbohydrates: 4g Protein: 16g Fat: 19g Sat Fat: 8g Cholesterol: 66mg Fiber: 1g Sugar: 2g

60. AIR FRYER STEAK TIPS WITH CREAMY HORSERADISH

Prep Time 5 mins
Cook Time 10 mins
Total Time 15 mins
Servings 6

Ingredients

Steak Tips

- 454 g Steak Tips steak or steak tips, cut into ¾" pieces
- 60 ml Olive Oil
- 5 ml Seasoning your choice
- Salt and Pepper to taste

Creamy Horseradish Sauce

- 180 g Prepared Horseradish
- 115 g Mayonnaise
- 123 g Sour Cream
- 5 ml Apple Cider Vinegar
- 3 drops Tabasco Sauce
- 5 ml Lemon Juice
- Salt and Pepper to taste

Preparation

Steak Tips

1. Cut the beef into 3/4" pieces. In a bag, combine the olive oil, Seasoning, salt & Pepper. Add the steak tips and press to completely cover. There's no need to marinade them because they'll be lovely and soft.
2. Preheat the air fryer to 204 °C. Depending on your model, place the sliced steak on a tray or basket.
3. Cook for four minutes before flipping. Cook for another 4 mins or until the steak reaches the desired internal temperature.

Creamy Horseradish Sauce
1. Stir together all of the ingredients in a mixing basin.
2. Refrigerate in an airtight jar for up to two weeks.

Nutritional information
Calories: 239kcal Carbohydrates: 1g Protein: 15g Fat: 20g Saturated Fat: 6g Cholesterol: 46mg Sodium: 40mg Fiber: 1g Sugar: 1g

61. **TENDER AIR FRYER STEAK WITH GARLIC MUSHROOMS**

Prep Time 5 mins
Cook Time 15 mins
Total Time 20 mins
Servings: 2

Ingredients
- 15 ml Avocado Oil
- 454 g Ribeye Steaks
- 473 g Halved Fresh Mushrooms
- 2.5 ml Salt
- 2.5 ml Black Pepper
- 28 g Unsalted Butter (Melted)
- 3 Cloves Minced Garlic
- 1.25 g Red Pepper Flakes (Optional)
- Chopped Parsley (Optional Garnish)

Preparation
1. Preheat your Air Fryer for 4 mins at 204°C.
2. After patting the steaks dry, cut them into 1/2" cubes. Place the steak cubes in a large mixing basin.
3. Cut fresh mushrooms in half and combine them with the cubed steak in a large mixing basin.
4. Toss the steak bits and mushrooms with the melted butter, garlic, salt, Pepper, and red pepper flakes in a large mixing bowl.
5. Place the mixture in an equal, non-overlapping layer in an air fryer basket. (Depending on the model of your AirFryer, you may need to cook in batches.)
6. Air-fried, the steak and mushrooms for 7-15 minutes, flipping twice during this time. After 7 minutes, check the steak to determine whether it's done to your preference. Continue to cook as required if it's too pink.

7. For the finest flavour and texture, garnish with parsley and serve immediately.

Nutritional information
Calories: 663kcal Carbohydrates: 5g Protein: 49g Fat: 51g Saturated Fat: 22g Cholesterol: 168mg Sodium: 707mg Fiber: 1g Sugar: 2g

62. **CRISPY BRATS**

Prep Time: 5 minutes
Cook Time: 15 minutes
Serving: 4

Ingredients
- 4 (85 g) beef bratwursts

Preparation
1. Brats should be placed in the air fryer basket.
2. Set the timer for 15 minutes and raise the temperature to 190°C.
3. Serve hot.

Nutritional information
per serving calories: 286 protein: 11.8 g fiber: 0.0 g net carbohydrates: 0.0 g fat: 24.8 g sodium: 50 mg Carbohydrates: 0.0 g Sugar: 0.0 g

63. **BACON-WRAPPED HOT DOG**

Prep Time: 5 minutes
Cook Time: 10 minutes
Serving: 4

Ingredients
- 4 beef hot dogs
- 4 slices sugar-free bacon

Preparation
1. Bacon slices are wrapped around each hot dog and fastened with toothpicks. Place it in your air fryer basket.
2. Set the timer for 10 minutes and raise the temperature to 187°C.
3. Each hot dog is turned over halfway through cooking. Bacon will be crispy when fully cooked. Serve hot.

Nutritional information
per serving calories: 197 protein: 9.2 g fiber: 0.0 g net carbohydrates: 1.3 g fat: 15.0 g sodium: 571 mg Carbohydrates: 1.3 g Sugar: 0.6 g

PORK RECIPE

64. BREADED PORK CHOPS

Prep Time: 10 minutes
Cook Time: 15 minutes
Serving 4

Ingredients
- 42 g pork rinds, finely ground
- 5 ml chili powder
- 2.5 ml garlic powder
- 15 ml coconut oil, melted
- 4 (113 g) pork chops

Preparation
1. Combine ground pork rinds, chili powder, and garlic powder in a large bowl.
2. Each pork chop should be brushed with coconut oil before being pressed into the pork rind mixture to cover both sides. Put the air fryer basket with each coated pork chop inside.
3. Set the timer for 15 minutes and raise the temperature to 204°C.
4. Each pork chop is turned over halfway during cooking.
5. The pork chops should be at least 63°C inside and have a golden exterior when fully cooked.

Nutritional information
per serving calories: 292 protein: 29.5 g fiber: 0.3 g net carbohydrates: 0.3 g fat: 18.5 g sodium: 268 mg Carbohydrates: 0.6 g Sugar: 0.1 g

65. PULLED PORK

Prep Time: 10 minutes
Cook Time: 2 1/2 hours
Serving: 8

Ingredients
- 30 ml chilli powder
- 5 ml garlic powder
- 2.5 ml onion powder
- 2.5 ml ground black pepper
- 2.5 ml cumin
- 1 (1.8 kg) pork shoulder

Preparation
1. In a small bowl, combine chilli powder, garlic powder, onion powder, pepper, and cumin. Pat the spice mixture into the skin of the pork shoulder. Fill the air fryer basket halfway with pork shoulder.
2. Set the air fryer temperature to 176°C and the timer for 150 minutes.

3. When done, the pork skin will be crispy, and the meat will shred readily with two forks. The interior temperature should be at least 63 degrees Celsius.

Nutritional information
calories: 537 protein: 42.6 g fiber: 0.8 g net carbohydrates: 0.7 g fat: 35.5 g sodium: 180 mg Carbohydrates: 1.5 g Sugar: 0.2 g

66. PIGS IN A BLANKET

Prep Time: 10 minutes
Cook Time: 7 minutes
Serving: 2

Ingredients
- 85 g shredded mozzarella cheese
- 14 g blanched finely ground almond flour
- 28 g full-fat cream cheese
- 2 (56 g) beef smoked sausages
- 2.5 g sesame seeds

Preparation
1. Mix the mozzarella, almond flour, and cream cheese in a large microwave-safe mixing bowl—microwave for 45 seconds, stirring halfway through, until smooth. Form the dough into ball, then cut it in half.
2. Each side should be pressed into a 4"- 5" rectangle. Roll one sausage in each half of the dough and seal the seams. Sesame seeds should be sprinkled on top.
3. Fill the air fryer basket with each wrapped sausage.
4. Set the air fryer temperature to 204°C and the timer for 7 minutes.
5. When fully cooked, the outside will be golden.
6. Serve right away.

Nutritional information
per serving calories: 405 protein: 17.5 g fiber: 0.8 g net carbohydrates: 2.1 g fat: 32.2 g sodium: 693 mg Carbohydrates: 2.9 g Sugar: 1.0 g

67. CRISPY PORK CHOP SALAD

Prep Time: 15 minutes
Cook Time: 8 minutes
Serving: 2

Ingredients
- 15 ml coconut oil
- 2 (113 g) pork chops, chopped into 1" cubes
- 10 ml chilli powder
- 5 ml paprika
- 2.5 ml garlic powder
- 1.25 ml onion powder
- 188 g chopped romaine
- 1 medium Roma tomato, diced
- 56 g shredded Monterey jack cheese
- 1 medium avocado, peeled, pitted, and diced
- 60 ml full-fat ranch dressing
- 4 g chopped cilantro

Preparation
1. Drizzle coconut oil over the meat in a large mixing basin. Season with chilli powder, paprika, garlic powder, and onion powder to taste. Insert the pork into the air fryer basket.
2. Set the air fryer temperature to 204°C and the timer for 8 minutes.
3. When the pork is thoroughly cooked, it will be golden and crispy.
4. Place the romaine, tomato, and crispy pork in a large mixing basin—shredded cheese and avocado on top. Toss the salad with the ranch dressing to coat it evenly.
5. Garnish with cilantro. Serve right away.

Nutritional information
pre serving calories: 526 protein: 34.4 g fiber: 8.6 g net carbohydrates: 5.2 g fat: 37.0 g sodium: 354 mg Carbohydrates: 13.8 g Sugar: 3.1 g

68. AIR FRYER SAUSAGE PATTIES

Prep Time 2 mins
Cook Time 8 mins
Total Time 10 mins
Servings: 4

Ingredients
- 227 g ground pork
- 5 ml minced onion
- 2.5 ml garlic powder
- 2.5 ml salt
- 1.25 ml pepper

Preparation
1. Preheat your air fryer to 204 °C.
2. Combine the meat and spices. Make four patties.
3. Put the patties in the air fryer basket. Air fry for 8 minutes

Nutritional information
per serving Calories: 155 Carbohydrates: 1.4g Protein: 9.8g Fat: 12g Cholesterol: 40.8mg Fiber: 0.2g Sugar: 0.5g

69. AIR FRYER BONE-IN PORK CHOPS RECIPES

Prep Time 5 minutes
Cook Time 12 minutes
Total Time 17 minutes
Servings: 2

Ingredients
- 680 g thick-cut bone-in pork chops
- 15 ml Cajun seasoning
- Salt and pepper to taste

Preparation
1. Brush both sides of the pork chops with olive oil and season with Cajun spice, salt, and pepper to taste.
2. Cook the pork in the air fryer basket for 8-12 minutes, flipping halfway through, or until an instant-read thermometer put into the thickest section reads 63 °C.
3. Place the pork on a platter and tent it with foil to keep it warm.

Nutrition Information:
Per Serving: Calories: 481 Total Fat: 25g Saturated Fat: 8g Trans Fat: 0g Unsaturated Fat: 13g Cholesterol: 191mg Sodium: 898mgCarbohydrates: 1gFiber: 0gSugar: 0gProtein: 58g

70. AIR FRYER SPARE RIBS

Prep Time 2 mins
Cook Time 30 mins
Total Time 32 mins
Servings: 4

Ingredients
- 907 g spare ribs
Smoked Paprika Rub
- 5 ml garlic powder
- 5 ml onion powder
- 5 ml smoked paprika
- 2.5 ml salt

Preparation

1. Preheat your air fryer to 204 °C. Coat the basket and rack in cooking spray.
2. Combine the rub ingredients and massage over the ribs.
3. Cook the ribs in the air fryer for 15 minutes.
4. Flip. Cook for another 15 minutes.

Nutritional information

per serving Calories: 445.4kcal Carbs: 1.2g Protein: 24.8g Fat: 37.2g Sat Fat: 12g Cholesterol: 127mg Sodium: 420.4mg Fiber: 0.3g Sugar: 0.1g

71.   THE PERFECT PORK TENDERLOIN IN AIR FRYER

Prep Time 5 mins
Cook Time 25 mins
Total Time 30 mins
Servings: 2-3

Ingredients

- 5 ml minced garlic
- 5 ml minced ginger
- 5 ml dried rosemary
- 5 ml dried oregano
- 454 g pork tenderloin
- Salt and pepper to taste

Preparation

1. Preheat the air fryer for 10 mins at 204°C.
2. Set aside the garlic, ginger, rosemary, and oregano in a small bowl.
3. Using a paper towel, pat dry the tenderloin and season with salt and pepper to taste. Rub the pork tenderloin with the mixture.
4. Insert the meat into the air fryer basket. Preheat the air fryer to 204 °C for 25 minutes or until an instant meat thermometer inserted into the middle reads 145°F.
5. Remove from the basket and cover with foil for 5-10 minutes before slicing.

Nutrition Information:

per serving Calories: 227 Fat: 6g Saturated Fat: 2g Trans Fat: 0g Cholesterol: 110mg Sodium: 87mg Carbohydrates: 1g Fiber: 0g Sugar: 0g Protein: 40g

72.   CRISPY AIR FRYER PORK BELLY

Prep Time 10 mins
Cook Time 45 mins
Total Time 55 mins
Servings: 4

Ingredients

- 680 g pork belly
- 10 ml sea salt
- 5 ml black pepper
- 2.5 ml bicarbonate of soda
- 2.5 ml garlic powder
- Oil for spraying

Preparation

1. Cut the pork belly into 1-inch strips or pieces the night before cooking, then place in a large mixing basin.
2. Sprinkle salt on the pork belly and massage it into the skin and flesh.
3. Place the pork on a large platter, skin side up, and season with black pepper.
4. Allow the pork belly to cool overnight in the refrigerator, uncovered.
5. In a small mixing bowl, combine the bicarbonate of soda and garlic powder. Rub the pork belly with the mixture.
6. Preheat the air fryer to 120° C.
7. Cooking oil spray the interior basket of the air fryer. Next, liberally spray the pork belly with cooking oil spray, ensuring the dry mixture is well wet.
8. Cook the pork belly in your air fryer basket in one layer, skin side up, for 25 minutes.
9. Increase the heat to 204°C and continue to air fry for another 20 minutes. Continue to increase time in 5-minute increments until the skin is crisped to your preference.

Nutrition Information:

per serving Calories: 529 Fat: 39g saturated Fat: 14g cholesterol: 143mg sodium: 972mg carbohydrates: 1g fiber: 0g sugar: 0g protein: 39g

73.   EASY AIR FRYER PORK CHOPS

Prep Time: 5 mins
Cook Time: 8 mins
Additional Time: 5 mins
Total Time: 18 Minutes
Servings: 4

Ingredients

- 4 boneless pork chops ¾-1 inch thick
- 30 ml olive oil
- 15 ml brown sugar
- 5 ml dried thyme
- 5 ml dried mustard
- 5 ml garlic powder
- 2.5 ml sea salt

- 2.5 ml fresh ground pepper

Preparation

1. Preheat the air fryer for 5 minutes @ 204°C.
2. Drizzle or brush the oil on all sides of the pork chops while the air fryer is preheating.
3. In a small bowl, combine the sugar, spices, salt, and pepper and sprinkle on both sides of pork chops.
4. Return the air fryer basket to the fryer and place the pork chops in a single layer.
5. Preheat the air fryer to 204°C for 8 minutes.
6. Flip the pork chops halfway through.
7. When the timer goes off, take the pork chops out of the air fryer and lay them on a dish. When checked using a meat thermometer, the pork chops should read 63°C. If they aren't finished, add another minute or two. Cover with foil and let aside for 5-10 minutes to rest.
8. Serve with the foil removed.
9. Any juices that have run out while resting can be saved and served on the side.

Nutritional information

per serving Calories: 391kcal Carbohydrates: 4g Protein: 37g Fat: 26g Saturated Fat: 8g Cholesterol: 103mg Sodium: 422mg Sugar: 3g

74. AIR FRYER HONEY MUSTARD PORK CHOPS

Prep Time: 15 Minutes
Cook Time: 15 Minutes
Total Time: 30 Minutes
Servings: 4.

Ingredients

- 4 pork chops boneless, thick cut
- 30 ml yellow mustard
- 5 ml salt
- 5 ml black pepper
- 2.5 ml smoked paprika
- 5 ml garlic powder
- 2 Cloves garlic crushed
- 60 ml honey
- 60 ml mustard stone ground
- 60 ml mayonnaise
- 1 lemon juiced
- 15 ml olive oil
- 15 g parsley chopped for garnish

Preparation

1. Take out the pork chops from the refrigerator and set aside for 15 minutes to come to room temperature.
2. Preheat your air fryer for 5 mins at 204 °C.
3. Brush the pork chops with a coating of yellow mustard—season with salt, black pepper, & smoked paprika on both sides.

4. Put the pork chops in your air fryer basket, allowing space between them. Cook for 8 minutes, then turn and cook for another 7 minutes.
5. Prepare the honey mustard while the pork chops are cooking. Combine honey, stone-ground mustard, mayonnaise, lemon juice, olive oil, garlic powder, and smashed garlic in a small bowl. To blend, whisk everything together. In a pan over high heat, combine the honey mustard combination. Cook, often stirring, for 5 minutes.
6. Let the pork chop rest for 5 mins on a chopping board. Garnish the pork chops with fresh chopped parsley and honey mustard.

Nutritional information

per serving Calories: 430kcal Carbohydrates: 23g Protein: 31g Fat: 24g Saturated Fat: 5g Cholesterol: 96mg Sodium: 1001mg Fiber: 2g Sugar: 19g

75. AIR FRYER PORK LOIN

Prep Time 5 mins
Cook Time 35 mins
Additional Time 5 mins
Total Time 45 mins
Servings: 6

Ingredients

- 1.3 kg pork loin roast
- 5 ml dried Italian seasoning
- 2.5 ml garlic powder
- 2.5 ml onion powder
- 2.5 ml sea salt
- 2.5 ml black pepper

Preparation

1. Preheat your air fryer to 187°C.
2. Mix the Italian seasoning, garlic powder, onion powder, salt, and pepper in a mixing bowl.
3. Trim any extra fat from the exterior of the pork loin before rubbing it all over with the spice mixture.
4. Cook the pork loin in the air fryer for 35 to 40 mins,* turning once halfway through, or until the roast reaches an internal temperature of 63°C.
5. Transfer the pork loin to a chopping board after removing it from the air fryer. Allow it to rest for about 5 mins before slicing and serving.

Nutrition Information:

per servings Calories: 438 total Fat: 20g saturated Fat: 6g cholesterol: 181mg sodium: 210mg carbohydrates: 1g fiber: 0g sugar: 0g protein: 60g

Prep Time 1 min
Cook Time 10 mins
Total Time 11 mins
Servings: 4

Ingredients

- 4-5 Italian sausage links
- parchment paper (optional)

Preparation

1. Place the sausage links in the air fryer basket. Line the bottom of the air fryer basket with parchment paper to catch any grease.
2. Air-fried for 10-12 minutes at 204°C or until golden brown on the exterior and juicy on the inside. When thoroughly cooked, the internal temperature of uncooked sausages should be 63°C. As desired, serve hot.

Nutrition Information:

per servings Calories: 323 Fat: 26g saturated Fat: 10g cholesterol: 53mg sodium: 697mg carbohydrates: 4g fiber: 0g sugar: 2g protein: 18g

Prep Time 5 mins
Cook Time 20 mins
Total Time 25 mins
Servings: 4

Ingredients

- 4 thick-cut pork chops
- 45 ml avocado oil or melted butter
- 5 ml paprika
- 5 ml onion powder
- 2.5 ml black pepper
- 5 ml garlic powder
- 5 ml salt
- 1 medium broccoli head
- 2 garlic cloves minced

Preparation

1. In a small bowl, combine paprika, black pepper, onion powder, garlic powder, and salt.
2. Drizzle oil over the pork chops and season on both sides with the spice mix (reserve 5 ml of seasoning for the broccoli).
3. Preheat your Air Fryer to 180 C, place the pork chops in the basket and cook for 10 minutes. Flip midway through. Cooking time should be increased to 14-16 minutes if the pork chops are thicker. The interior temperature of fully cooked pork chops is 63 degrees Celsius.
4. In the meantime, chop the broccoli into small florets and place them in a basin. Toss the remaining seasoning mix, garlic, and oil/butter to coat.
5. Cook the broccoli in the air fryer basket for 7 minutes at 204°C. Flip midway through.
6. Serve the pork chops with a dab of flavoured butter on top. Enjoy!

Nutritional information

per servings Calories: 352kcal Carbs: 10g Protein: 33g Fat: 20g Saturated Fat: 5g Cholesterol: 90mg Fiber: 4g Sugar: 3g Net Carbs: 6g

LAMB RECIPE

78.   LAMB SHANKS AND CARROTS

Prep time: 10 minutes
Cooking time: 45 minutes
Servings: 4

Ingredients:
- 4 lamb shanks
- 30 ml olive oil
- 1 yellow onion, finely chopped
- 6 carrots, roughly chopped
- 2 garlic cloves, minced
- 30 ml tomato paste
- 5 ml oregano, dried
- 1 tomato, roughly chopped
- 30 ml water
- 360 ml red wine
- Salt and black pepper to the taste

Preparation
1. Season the lamb with salt & pepper, massage with oil, and cook for 10 minutes at 182 °C in an air fryer.
2. Toss onion, carrots, garlic, tomato paste, oregano, wine, and water in a pan that fits your air fryer.
3. Toss the lamb, then place it in the air fryer for 35 minutes at 187° C.
4. Serve everything on individual plates.

Nutritional information:
Calories 432, fat 17, fibre 8, carbs 17, protein 43

79.   EASY LAMB KOFTA

Prep Time 15 mins
Cook Time 12 mins
Total Time 27 mins
Servings 6

Ingredients
- 907 g ground lamb (can sub beef)
- 2 cloves garlic, finely minced or pressed
- 8 g chopped fresh cilantro or parsley
- 15 ml ground coriander
- 15 ml ground cumin
- 5 ml paprika
- 7.5 ml salt
- 2.5 ml ground cassia
- 2.5 ml black pepper

Preparation
1. Soak bamboo skewers in water for about1 an hour before using.
2. Mix all ingredients in a large mixing basin and mix well with your hands. Make 12 oval-shaped logs, each about 1 inch broad and 4 inches long. Thread the logs onto the skewers if using.
3. Cook for 10 to 12 minutes at 204°C or until well browned and the centre of the kofta reaches at least 57°C for medium. Allow for a 5-minute pause before serving.
4. Grill the kofta over medium heat, rotating to brown evenly, or bake at 190°C.

Nutritional information
per servings Calories: 437kcal Carbohydrates: 1.8g Protein: 37.9g Fat: 27.4g Fiber: 0.8g

80.   LAMB AND CREAMY BRUSSELS SPROUTS

Prep time: 10 mins
Cook time: 1 hr and 10 mins
Servings: 4

Ingredients:
- 907 g leg of lamb scored
- 30 ml olive oil
- 2 g rosemary, chopped
- 15 ml lemon thyme, chopped
- 1 garlic clove, minced
- 680 g Brussels sprouts, trimmed
- 14 g butter, melted
- 118 ml sour cream
- Salt and black pepper to the taste

Preparation
1. Season the leg of lamb with salt, pepper, thyme, and rosemary, brush with oil and set it in the basket of your air fryer. Cook at 149 degrees C for 1 hour, then transfer to a platter and keep warm.
2. Toss Brussels sprouts with salt, pepper, garlic, butter, and sour cream in a pan that fits your air fryer, then place in the air fryer and cook at 204 degrees C for 10 minutes.
3. Serve the lamb on plates with Brussels sprouts on the side.

Nutritional information:
per servings Calories 440, fat 23, fibre 0, carbs 2, protein 49

81. MARINATED LAMB AND VEGGIES

Prep time: 10 minutes
Cook time: 30 minutes
Servings: 4

Ingredients:
- 1 carrot, chopped
- 1 onion, sliced
- 7.5 ml olive oil
- 85 g bean sprouts
- 266 g lamb loin, sliced

For the marinade:
- 1 garlic clove, minced
- ½ apple, grated
- Salt and black pepper to the taste
- 1 small yellow onion, grated
- 8 g ginger, grated
- 82 g soy sauce
- 12 g sugar
- 30 ml orange juice

Preparation
1. In a mixing bowl, combine 1 grated onion, apple, garlic, 8 g ginger, soy sauce, orange juice, sugar, and black pepper, stir well, and set aside for 10 minutes.
2. Heat the olive oil in a skillet that fits your air fryer over medium-high heat, then add 1 sliced onion, carrot, and bean sprouts, mix, and cook for 3 minutes.
3. Transfer the pan to your preheated air fryer and cook the lamb and marinade for 25 minutes at 182 °C.
4. Serve everything in separate bowls.

Nutritional information:
per servings Calories 265, fat 3, fibre 7, carbs 18, protein 22

82. CRISPY LAMB

Preparation time: 10 minutes
Cooking time: 30 minutes
Servings: 4

Ingredients:
- 7 g breadcrumbs
- 15 g macadamia nuts, toasted and crushed
- 15 ml olive oil
- 1 garlic clove, minced
- 793 g rack of lamb
- Salt and black pepper to the taste
- 1 egg,
- 3 g rosemary, chopped

Preparation
1. In a mixing dish, combine the oil and garlic.
2. Season the lamb with salt & pepper, then brush with oil.
3. In a separate bowl, combine the nuts, breadcrumbs, and rosemary.
4. In a separate dish, whisk the egg well.
5. Dip lamb in egg, then in macadamia mixture, then place in the air fryer basket, cook at 182°C for 25 minutes, then raise heat to 204 °C for 5 minutes longer.
6. Serve immediately on individual plates.

Nutritional information:
per servings Calories 230, fat 2, fibre 2, carbs 10, protein 12

83. LAMB AND GREEN PESTO

Prep time: 1 hr
Cook time: 45 mins
Servings: 4

Ingredients:
- 61 g parsley
- 30 g mint
- 1 small yellow onion, roughly chopped
- 42 g pistachios, chopped
- 5 ml lemon zest, grated
- 75 ml olive oil
- Salt and black pepper to the taste
- 907 g lamb riblets
- ½ onion, chopped
- 5 garlic cloves, minced
- Juice from 1 orange

Preparation
1. Blend parsley, mint, onion, pistachios, lemon zest, salt, pepper, and oil in a food processor until smooth.
2. Rub this mixture over the lamb, place in a basin, cover, and chill for 1 hour.
3. Transfer the lamb to a baking dish that fits your air fryer, add the garlic, pour with orange juice, and cook for 45 minutes at 149 °C.
4. Serve the lamb on individual plates.
5. Enjoy!

Nutritional information:
per servings calories 200, fat 4, fibre 6, carbs 15, protein 7

Prep Time 5 minutes
Cook Time 12 minutes
Total Time 17 minutes
Servings: 4

Ingredients

- 454 g ground lamb
- 5 ml ground cumin
- 4.5 g granulated onion
- 7.5 g fresh parsley
- 1.25 ml ground cassia
- Salt and pepper

Preparation

1. Combine the lamb, cumin, onion, parsley, and cassia in a large mixing basin. Mix until all of the ingredients are uniformly distributed.
2. Form the mixture into 1-inch balls.
3. Cook the lamb meatballs in the air fryer basket for 12-15 minutes at 176°C. Halfway through, shake the meatballs.

Nutrition Information:

per servings Calories: 328 Fat: 22g Saturated Fat: 9g
Cholesterol: 110mg Sodium: 95mg Carbohydrates: 1g Fiber:
0g Sugar: 0g Protein: 28g

Prep Time: 15 mins
Cook Time: 5–7 mins
Servings: 4

Ingredients:

Dressing:
- 285 g plain Greek yoghurt
- 15 ml. lemon juice
- 5 ml dried dill weed, crushed
- 5 ml ground oregano
- 2.5 ml. salt

Meatballs:
- 227 g ground lamb
- 3 g diced onion
- 5 ml dried parsley
- 5 ml dried dill weed, crushed
- 1.25 ml oregano
- 1.25 ml coriander
- 1.25 ml ground cumin
- 1.25 ml. salt
- 4 pita halves optional

Toppings:

- Crumbled feta cheese, Sliced black olives, Chopped fresh peppers, Slivered Seedless cucumber, Red onion, thinly sliced.

Preparation

1. While cooking the lamb, chill the dressing ingredients.
2. Combine all meatball ingredients in a mixing bowl and whisk to distribute seasonings.
3. Form the beef mixture into 12 little meatballs, which can be spherical or slightly flattened.
4. Air fry at 198°C for 5 to 7 minutes or until thoroughly done. Remove from the air fryer and blot dry with paper towels.
5. Fill pita pockets with meatballs and your preferred toppings, then top with dressing.

Nutritional information

per servings Calories: 270 Fat: 15 g Protein: 18 g Carbs: 17 g
Fiber: 2 g Sugar: 2 g Sodium: 618 mg

Prep Time: 30 mins
Cook Time: 20 mins
Servings: 2-3

Ingredients:

- 10 ml oil
- 2.5 ml ground rosemary
- 2.5 ml lemon juice
- 454 g lamb chops, approximately 1-inch thick
- Salt and pepper to taste
- Cooking spray

Preparation

1. Rub the oil, rosemary, and lemon juice mixture over the lamb chops. Season to taste with salt and pepper.
2. Allow the lamb chops to rest in the refrigerator for 15 to 20 minutes for the best flavour.
3. Coat your air fryer basket with nonstick spray before adding the lamb chops.
4. Air-fried at 182°C for around 20 minutes. The chops will be cooked to medium rare. The meat should be juicy but not pink. Air fry for 1 to 2 mins longer for well-done chops. Cook for another 12 minutes to achieve rare chops.

Nutritional information

per servings Calories: 237 Fat: 12 g Protein: 30 g Carbs: 0 g
Fiber: 0 g Sugar 0 g Sodium: 115 mg

Prep Time: 40 mins
Cook Time: 20 mins
Servings: 4

Ingredients:

- 454 lamb sirloin steaks, pastured, boneless

For the Marinade:

- 1/2 white onion, peeled
- 5 ml ground fennel
- 5 garlic cloves, peeled
- 4 slices ginger
- 5 ml salt
- 2.5 ml ground cardamom
- 5 ml. garam masala
- 5 ml ground cassia
- 5 ml cayenne pepper

Preparation

1. Combine all marinade ingredients in a food processor and pulse until well mixed.
2. Cut the lamb chops with a knife, then combine them with the marinade in a large mixing basin.
3. After fully covering the lamb chops with the marinade, place them in the refrigerator for at least 30 minutes.
4. Then, turn on the air fryer, place the frying basket inside, coat it with olive oil, seal the lid, and warm for 5 minutes at 165°C.
5. Open the fryer, drop the lamb chops inside, close the lid, and cook for 15 minutes, or until the steaks are delightfully brown and cooked, turning halfway through.
6. Remove the lamb steaks to a platter and serve when the air fryer beeps.

Nutritional information :

per servings Calories: 181 Carbs: 3 g Fat: 7 g Protein: 23 g Fiber: 1 g

Prep time: 5 mins
Cook time: 7 mins
Total time: 12 mins

Ingredients 4 serving

- 4 lamb chops
- 30 ml olive oil
- 8 g minced garlic
- 2.5 g fresh basil
- 15 ml oregano
- 2.5 ml ground pepper
- 2.5 ml salt
- fresh thyme for garnish

Preparation

1. To begin, put all ingredients in a large Ziplock bag except the fresh thyme. Shake the bag to coat the lamb chops equally with the olive oil and spices.
2. At this point, either preheat the air fryer to 204 degrees Celsius and air fry immediately or place the Ziplock bag in the refrigerator for up to 24 hours to marinate.
3. Place the lamb chops in your air fryer basket or on the air fryer pan after preheating the air fryer.
4. 7–10 minutes in an air fryer. After 7 minutes, use a meat thermometer to check the internal temperature of the meat and add further air frying time if required.
5. Finally, after the meat has reached the desired temperature, take it from the air fryer.
6. Allow the meat to rest for 5 mins before serving and slicing.
7. Garnish with fresh thyme if preferred.

Nutritional information

per servings calories: 353kcal, carbohydrates: 2g, Protein: 42g, fat: 15g, saturated fat: 6g, fibre: 1g, sugar: 1g,

Prep Time: 1 hr 10 mins
Cook Time: 13 mins
Servings: 4

Ingredients:
- 454 g lamb chops, pastured

For the Marinate:
- 2 tbsp. lemon juice
- 5 ml dried rosemary
- 5 ml salt
- 5 ml dried thyme
- 5 ml. coriander
- 5 ml dried oregano
- 30 ml olive oil

Preparation
1. To create the marinade, whisk together all of the ingredients in a mixing basin.
2. Pour the marinade into a large plastic bag, add the lamb chops, seal the bag, and turn the bag upside down to coat the lamb chops with the marinade. Refrigerate for about an hour before serving.
3. Then, turn on the air fryer, insert the fryer basket, coat it with olive oil, seal the lid, and warm for 5 minutes at 198 degrees Celsius.
4. Open the fryer, add the marinated lamb chops, close the lid, and cook for 8 minutes or until delightfully brown and done, flipping halfway through.
5. When the air fryer beeps, transfer the lamb chops to a serving dish and serve.

Nutritional information :
per servings Calories: 177 Carbs: 1.7 g Fat: 8 g Protein: 23 g Fiber: 0.5 g

Prep time: 10 mins
Cook time: 45 mins
Servings: 4

Ingredients:
- 4 lamb shanks
- 1 yellow onion, chopped
- 15 ml olive oil
- 7 g coriander seeds, crushed
- 8 g plain flour
- 4 bay leaves
- 10 ml honey
- 142 g dry sherry
- 600 ml chicken stock
- Salt and pepper to the taste

Preparation
1. Season the lamb shanks with salt & pepper, rub with half of the oil, and cook for 10 minutes at 182 degrees Celsius in an air fryer.
2. Heat the remaining oil in a pan that fits your air fryer over medium-high heat; add the onion and coriander, mix, and cook for 5 minutes.
3. Stir in the flour, sherry, stock, honey, bay leaves, salt, and pepper, and bring to a simmer. Add the lamb and cook at 182 degrees C for 30 minutes.
4. Serve everything on individual plates.

Nutritional information:
per servings Calories 283, fat 4, fibre 2, carbs 17, protein 26

Preparation time: 10 minutes
Cooking time: 35 minutes
Servings: 6

Ingredients:
- 12 g ginger, grated
- 2 garlic cloves, minced
- 4 g cardamom, ground
- 1 red onion, chopped
- 454 g lamb meat, cubed
- 10 ml cumin powder
- 5 ml garam masala
- 2.5 ml chilli powder
- 2.5 ml turmeric
- 10 ml coriander, ground
- 454 g spinach
- 397 g canned tomatoes, chopped

Preparation
1. Mix lamb with spinach, tomatoes, ginger, garlic, onion, cardamom, cloves, cumin, garam masala, chile, turmeric, and coriander in a heatproof dish that fits your air fryer, swirl, and cook at 182 degrees C for 35 minutes.
2. Serve in individual bowls.

Nutritional information:
per servings Calories 160, fat 6, fibre 3, carbs 17, protein 20

POULTRY RECIPE

92. CHICKEN PIZZA CRUST

Prep Time: 10 minutes
Cook Time: 25 minutes
Serving: 4

Ingredients:
- 454 g ground chicken thigh meat
- 22 g grated Parmesan cheese
- 112 g shredded mozzarella

Preparation
1. Combine all ingredients in a large bowl. Divide into four equal pieces.
2. Each piece of the chicken mixture should be spread out onto one of the four parchment circles that are 6" in diameter. Working in batches as necessary, place into the air fryer basket.
3. Set the timer for 25 minutes and raise the temperature to 190°C.
4. Halfway through the cooking process, flip the crust.
5. When it is thoroughly cooked, you may add cheese and your preferred toppings and cook for an additional five minutes. Or you may freeze or refrigerate the crust and top it until you're ready to eat.

Nutritional information:
per serving calories: 230 protein: 24.7 g fiber: 0.0 g net carbohydrates: 1.2 g fat: 12.8 g sodium: 268 mg Carbohydrates: 1.2 g Sugar: 0.2 g

93. BEST AIR FRYER CHICKEN FAJITAS RECIPE

Prep Time 10 minutes
Cook Time 15 minutes
Total Time 25 minutes
Servings: 4

Ingredients
- 454 g Boneless, skinless chicken breast
- 15 ml olive oil
- 15 ml fajita seasoning
- 2 Red peppers seeded and thinly sliced
- 1 big onion, thinly sliced
- 15 g chopped fresh cilantro
- one jalapeno pepper, seeded and thinly sliced (optional)
- 15 ml lime juice
- 8 (6 inches) tortillas (your favourite) warmed
- Desired toppings

Preparation
1. Cut the chicken into thin strips and combine it with the olive oil, fajita spice, bell pepper, and onion in a big zip-top plastic bag or large mixing bowl. Close the bag and begin coating. Refrigerate for at least 30 mins and up to 8 hrs.
2. Preheat the air fryer to 198°C for 5 minutes.
3. Spread the chicken mixture in the air fryer basket and cook for 15 mins, or until the chicken is cooked through and the veggies are soft. Shake the basket halfway through.
4. In a mixing bowl, combine the cooked chicken, jalapeño, cilantro, and lime juice. Serve with tortillas of your choice and chosen toppings. Enjoy!

Nutrition Information:
per servings Calories: 240 Fat: 8g Saturated Fat: 2g Cholesterol: 96mg Sodium: 240mg Carbohydrates: 5g Fiber: 1g Sugar: 2g Protein: 36g

94. EASY AIR FRYER CHICKEN THIGHS BONE-IN, SKIN-ON

Prep Time 5 mins
Cook Time 24 mins
Total Time 29 mins
Servings: 2-4

Ingredients
- 680 g bone-in, skin-on chicken thighs
- 5 ml minced garlic
- 5 ml chopped fresh sage
- 5 ml chopped fresh rosemary
- 5 ml melted unsalted butter
- Salt and black Pepper to taste

Preparation
1. Pat the chicken dry with paper towel, then season with garlic, sage, rosemary, butter, salt, and Pepper and toss to mix.
2. Place the chicken thighs skin side down in the air fryer basket; cook at 193 °C for 12 minutes on each side, or until the meat thermometer inserted in the thickest section of the chicken without touching the bone registers 64 °C.
3. Serve the chicken with your favourite side dishes.

Nutrition Information:
per servings Calories: 252 Fat: 17g Saturated Fat: 5g Cholesterol: 148mg Sodium: 198mg Carbs: 0g Fiber: 0g Sugar: 0g Protein: 27g

95. PECAN CRUSTED CHICKEN | LOW CARB PECAN CHICKEN
     RECIPE

Prep Time: 5 mins
Cook Time: 12 mins
Total Time: 17 mins
Servings: 4

Ingredients
- 453.59 g chicken tenders
- 5 ml Sea Salt
- 5 ml Ground Black Pepper
- 2.5 ml Smoked Paprika
- 62.25 g Coarse-Ground Mustard
- 30 ml Sugar-Free Maple Syrup or honey
- 80 g finely-crushed pecans

Preparation
1. In a large bowl, put the chicken tenders.
2. Mix in the salt, Pepper, and smoked paprika until the chicken is completely covered.
3. Mix in the honey and mustard well.
4. On a dish, scatter the finely smashed pecans.
5. Roll the chicken tenders in the crushed pecans, one at a time, until both sides are covered. Remove any excess with a brush.
6. Place the tenders in your air fryer basket and repeat until all tenders have been coated and placed in the air fryer basket.
7. Heat the air fryer to 176 °C for 12 minutes, or until the chicken is cooked through and the pecans are golden brown.

Nutritional information
per servings Calories: 325kcal Carbohydrates: 8g Protein: 27g Fat: 21g Fiber: 3g Sugar: 3g

96. AIR FRYER FRENCH ONION CHICKEN BREAST AND
     FONTINA CHEESE

Prep Time 10 mins
Cook Time 10 mins
Additional Time 10 mins
Total Time 30 mins
Servings: 2

Ingredients
Roasted Onions:
- 1 onion
- 30 ml olive oil
- 5 ml sugar
- salt and Pepper to taste

Chicken:
- 2 boneless, skinless chicken breast
- 10 ml olive oil
- salt and Pepper to taste
- 85 g Fontina cheese, sliced

Preparation
1. To begin, cut the onions into thin slices.
2. In a small bowl, toss the sliced onions with olive oil, sugar, salt, and Pepper. Then, place the coated onions in the air fryer basket and cook for 5-7 minutes at 176 °C
3. Coat chicken breast with olive oil, season with salt & pepper, then air fry for 7-9 minutes at 176 °C
4. Serve the chicken with the caramelised onions on top.
5. Place the caramelised onions in the air fryer for about 1-2 minutes at 176 °C, air fryer setting, or until the cheese is melted.
6. Serve, and have fun!

Nutrition Information:
per servings Calories: 717 Fat: 49g saturated Fat: 20g cholesterol: 201mg sodium: 1066mg carbohydrates: 8g fiber: 1g sugar: 6g protein: 60g

97. BEST AIR FRYER TURKEY BREAST RECIPE

Prep Time 10 mins
Cook Time 45 mins
Total Time 55 mins

Ingredients
- 4 large sage leaves
- 15 g fresh parsley
- 15 ml fresh thyme leaves
- 5 ml fresh rosemary
- 57 g butter, melted
- 1 (2.3 kg) turkey breast, ribs removed
- Salt and Pepper to taste

Preparation
1. Chop the herbs finely (sage, parsley, thyme, and rosemary). Stir together the chopped herbs and melted butter in a small dish.
2. Pat turkey breast dry with paper towel, season with salt and black Pepper, and then season with the herb butter mixture under the skin and all over.
3. Put the turkey breast in the air fryer basket, skin side down, and cook for 25 minutes at 176 °C. Flip and cook for another 20 mins on the side or until the meat thermometer inserted in the thickest section marks 174 °C.

4. Remove from the air fryer and set aside for 10 to 15 minutes before cutting.

Nutrition Information:

per servings Calories: 68 Fat: 7g Saturated Fat: 4g Cholesterol: 20mg Sodium: 88mg Carbs: 0g Fiber: 0g Sugar: 0g Protein: 1g

98. CORNISH HEN IN AIR FRYER (SUPER EASY)

Prep Time 10 mins
Cook Time 30 mins
Total Time 40 mins
Serving: 2

Ingredients

- 5 ml onion powder
- 5 ml garlic powder
- 5 ml paprika
- 2.5 ml dry rosemary
- 2.5 ml dry thyme
- 1 (907 g) Cornish hen
- 15 ml olive oil or avocado oil
- Salt and Pepper to taste

Preparation

1. Preheat your air fryer for 5 mins at 193 °C.
2. Set aside the onion powder, garlic powder, paprika, rosemary, and thyme in a small bowl.
3. Using a paper towel, pat dry the cornish hen. Season the Cornish hen with salt and Pepper to taste, including the cavity, and then apply the spice blend all over the chicken, including the cavities and below the skin.
4. Cook the cornish game fowl in the air fryer basket for 20 minutes breast side down and 10 minutes breast side up at 193°C. The cornish hen should be cooked until the internal temperature is 74 °C.
5. Allow the Cornish hen to rest for 10 minutes before slicing. Enjoy

Nutrition Information:

per servings Calories: 135 Total Fat: 14g Saturated Fat: 2g Cholesterol: 0mg Sodium: 3mg Carbohydrates: 3g Fiber: 1g Sugar: 0g Protein: 1g

99. AIR FRYER FROZEN CHICKEN BREAST

Prep Time 5 minutes
Cook Time 15 minutes
Total Time 20 minutes
Serving: 1

Ingredients

- 1 skinless and boneless chicken breast

- 5 ml olive oil
- 5 ml - 21 salute seasoning(or your favourite salt-free Seasoning)
- Salt and Pepper

Preparation

1. Coat the chicken breast with olive oil using a silicone brush, season with salt & Pepper to taste on both sides, then sprinkle with 21 salute seasoning on both sides.
2. Place the chicken breast in your air fryer basket and cook for the following time, depending on thickness:
   18 to 20 minutes at 190°C for 1/2-inch thick
   30 minutes at 190°C for 1 inch thick
   40 minutes at 190°C for 1 1/2-inch thick
   2" thick: 50 minutes at 190°C
1. Halfway through, turn the chicken breast (the cooking time depend on your chicken breast thickness, add extra mins if needed).
2. Once the chicken breast has reached an internal temperature of 74 °C, remove it from the air fryer basket and set it aside for 5 minutes before slicing.

Nutrition Information:

per servings Calories: 238 Total Fat: 9g Saturated Fat: 2g Cholesterol: 102mg Sodium: 89mg Carbohydrates: 0g Fiber: 0g Sugar: 0g Protein: 37g

100. AIR FRYER CHEESY BACON HASSELBACK CHICKEN

Prep Time: 10 mins
Cook Time: 15 mins
Total Time: 25 mins
Servings: 3

Ingredients

- 3 chicken breasts, skinless, boneless
- 4 Oz. cream cheese 1/2 block
- 56 g Colby jack cheese shredded
- 56 g pepper jack cheese shredded
- 60 g cheddar cheese shredded
- 56 g cooked bacon chopped
- 30 g spinach fresh, chopped
- 5 ml. garlic minced
- 5 ml. smoked paprika
- 2.5 ml. salt
- 2.5 ml. Pepper
- 112 g bocconcini mini mozzarella balls

Preparation

1. Cut 6 slits across the top of each chicken breast, being careful not to cut all the way through.

2. Combine all of the remaining ingredients, except the bocconcini, in a mixing bowl and stir thoroughly.
3. Fill each slit with the cheese mixture and sprinkle with bocconcini balls.
4. Spray each chicken breast with olive oil or nonstick cooking spray before placing it in the air fryer basket. Insert the basket into your air fryer.
5. Heat the air fryer to 182°C for 15 minutes. Check for doneness; if not fully cooked, cook for another minute or two.

Nutritional information

per servings Calories: 762kcal Carbohydrates: 5g Protein: 75g Fat: 48g Saturated Fat: 24g Trans Fat: 1g Cholesterol: 268mg Fiber: 1g Sugar: 2g

101. AIR FRYER SHREDDED CHICKEN

Prep Time 10 mins
Cook Time 45 mins
Total Time 55 mins
Servings: 4

Ingredients

- 1 Whole Chicken
- 15 ml Extra Virgin Olive Oil
- 15 ml Italian Seasoning
- Salt & Pepper

Preparation

1. Prepare the entire chicken. Tie the chicken legs together and lay them in the air fryer basket, breast side up. Season with salt, Pepper, and Italian Seasoning or mixed herbs after applying half of the oil to all visible skin.
2. Air-fried the chicken for 25 minutes at 180 degrees Celsius, then flip it over, oil, and season again. Then, at the same temperature, air fry for another 20 minutes.
3. Let the chicken cool before shredding it off the carcass with your hands. Remove all of the little bones from the shredded chicken.
4. Fill containers for the fridge or freezer, or use them in a dish that calls for leftover rotisserie chicken.

Nutritional information

per servings Calories: 444kcal Carbohydrates: 1g Protein: 36g Fat: 32g Saturated Fat: 9g Cholesterol: 143mg Fiber: 1g Sugar: 1g

102. AIR FRYER CHICKEN DRUMSTICKS

Prep Time: 5 Minutes
Cook Time: 25 Minutes
Total Time: 30 Minutes
Servings: 12

Ingredients

- 12 chicken drumsticks
- 30 ml olive oil
- 15 ml smoked paprika
- 5 ml garlic powder
- 5 ml dried mustard
- 5 ml dried parsley
- 2.5 ml onion powder
- 5 ml salt or half a teaspoon table salt

Preparation

1. In a large mixing basin, combine the chicken drumsticks. Toss in the olive oil to coat.
2. Toss the chicken in the basin with the spices until fully covered.
3. Arrange drumsticks in one single layer in the air fryer basket (a little bit of overlap is ok)
4. Set the air fryer to 193 °C and place the basket inside.
5. Cook for 22-25 minutes, rotating halfway through until the chicken is golden brown and the flesh is no longer pink. If you're using a meat thermometer, aim for 74°C.

Nutritional information

per servings Calories: 190kcal Carbohydrates: 1g Protein: 22g Fat: 11g Saturated Fat: 3g Cholesterol: 116mg Sodium: 284mg

103. AIR FRYER CHICKEN WINGS

Prep Time 5 mins
Cook Time 25 mins
Total Time 30 mins
Serving: 4

Ingredients

- 454 g chicken drumettes and flats
- salt and Pepper to taste
- One homemade recipe of buffalo sauce (optional)

Preparation

1. Preheat the air fryer to 193°C.
2. If necessary, trim or divide wings at the joint to create a flat drumette per chicken wing. Remove the tips.
3. Pat chicken wings dry; you want them as dry as possible to help them crisp up.

4. Season chicken wings with salt & Pepper.
5. Cook the wings at 193°C for 20-22 minutes, shaking the basket or turning the wings halfway through.
6. Increase the temperature of the air fryer to 204°C and cook until the chicken wings have a lovely crispy exterior, around 4-5 minutes.
7. Coat in homemade buffalo sauce or your favourite sauce.
8. Enjoy right now.

Nutrition Information:

per servings Calories: 315 Fat: 20g saturated Fat: 7g cholesterol: 124mg sodium: 340mg carbohydrates: 1g fiber: 0g sugar: 0g protein: 30g

104. LOW CARB KETO PALEO BAKED CHICKEN NUGGETS IN THE AIR FRYER

Prep Time 10 mins
Cook Time 15 mins
Total Time 25 mins
Servings 4

Ingredients

- 454 g Free-range boneless, skinless chicken breast
- Pinch sea salt
- 5 ml Sesame oil
- 28 g Coconut flour
- 2.5 ml Ground ginger
- 4 Egg whites
- 90 ml Toasted sesame seeds
- A cooking spray of choice

For the dip:

- 30 ml Natural creamy almond butter
- 20 ml Coconut aminos (or GF soy sauce)
- 15 ml Water
- 10 ml Rice vinegar
- 5 ml Sriracha, or to taste
- 2.5 ml Ground ginger
- 2.5 ml Monk Fruit (omit for whole30)

Preparation

1. Preheat your air fryer for 10 minutes at 204 °C.
2. While the air fryer warms up, chop the chicken into 1-inch nuggets, dry them off, and lay them in a bowl. Toss with the salt and sesame oil until evenly coated.
3. Shake up the coconut flour and ground ginger in a large Ziploc bag. Shake the chicken until it is evenly covered.
4. In a large mixing bowl, combine the egg whites and the chicken nuggets, swirling until completely coated.
5. Fill a big Ziploc bag halfway with sesame seeds. Shake out any extra egg from the chicken before adding the nuggets to the bag and shaking until fully covered.

6. Coat the mesh air fryer basket liberally with cooking spray. Place the nuggets in the basket, being careful not to crowd them, or they will not crisp up. Spritz with a little cooking spray.
7. Cook for 6 minutes. Cooking spray should be sprayed on both sides of each nugget. Cook for another 5-6 minutes or until the interior is no longer pink and the exterior is crispy.
8. While the nuggets are cooking, combine all of the sauce ingredients in a mixing bowl and whisk until smooth.
9. Serve the nuggets with the dip.

Nutritional information

per servings Calories: 286kcal Carbohydrates: 10.3g Protein: 29.9g Fat: 11.6g Saturated Fat: 1.2g Fiber: 5g Sugar: 1.5g

105. AIR FRYER LEMON PEPPER WINGS

Prep Time 5 mins
Cook Time 25 mins
Total Time 30 mins
Serving: 4

Ingredients

- 680 g chicken wings, drumettes and flats separated and tips discarded
- 10 ml lemon pepper seasoning
- 1.25 ml cayenne pepper

For The Lemon Pepper Sauce

- 43 g butter
- 5 ml lemon pepper seasoning
- 5 ml honey

Preparation

1. Preheat your air fryer to 193°C.
2. Season the chicken wings with lemon pepper and cayenne pepper.
3. Fill the air fryer, not more than halfway, with the lemon pepper wings. Cook the basket for 20-22 minutes, shaking halfway through.
4. Cook for a further 3-5 minutes at 204 °C to achieve a lovely crispy exterior on the chicken wings.
5. In a bowl, combine the melted butter, extra lemon pepper spice, and honey while the chicken wings are cooking.
6. Remove the chicken wings from your air fryer and cover them with lemon honey sauce. Enjoy!

Nutrition Information:

per servings Calories: 462 Fat: 36.2g saturated Fat: 12.6g cholesterol: 154mg sodium: 866mg carbohydrates: 2g fiber: 0g sugar: 1g protein: 31.2g

FISH AND SEAFOOD RECIPE

106. AIR FRYER SHRIMP RECIPE

Prep Time 5 min
Cook Time 10 min
Servings: 4

Ingredients

- 454 g large raw shrimp, peeled & deveined
- 5 ml minced garlic
- 14 g unsalted melted butter
- 5 ml lemon juice
- Salt and pepper to taste (optional)
- Chopped parsley to garnish

Preparation

1. Preheat your air fryer for 4 mins at 176 °C.
2. Toss the shrimp, garlic, butter, and lemon juice in a medium bowl to coat evenly.
3. Cook the shrimp in the air fryer basket for 8 to 10 minutes, depending on their size, shaking the basket or stirring halfway through.
4. Take out the shrimp from the air fryer and top with fresh parsley and lemon wedges. Enjoy!

Nutrition Information:

per servings Calories: 108 Fat: 4g Saturated Fat: 2g Cholesterol: 151mg Carbohydrates: 1g Fiber: 0g Sugar: 0g Protein: 16g

107. AIR FRYER MAHI MAHI RECIPE

Prep Time 5 min
Cook Time 10 min
Total Time 15 min
Serving: 2

Ingredients

- 2 (170 g) mahi-mahis, fresh or thawed.
- 15 ml taco seasoning
- Cooking spray, olive oil

Preparation

1. Pat the fish dry with paper towel; brush or spray the Mahi Mahi with olive oil; season on both sides with taco spice.
2. Cook the fish in the air fryer basket for 10 minutes, flipping halfway through or until opaque and flaky.
3. Serve and have fun!

Nutrition Information: Yield: 2 Serving Size: 1

per servings Calories: 161 Fat: 8g Saturated Fat: 1g Cholesterol: 75mg Sodium: 398mg Carbohydrates: 3g Fiber: 1g Sugar: 0g Protein: 19g

108. AIR FRYER HEALTHY WHITE FISH WITH GARLIC & LEMON

Prep Time 5 mins
Cook Time 12 mins
Total Time 17 mins
Servings: 2

Ingredients

- 340 g tilapia filets or other white fish (2 filets-6 ounces each)
- 2.5 ml garlic powder
- 2.5 ml lemon pepper seasoning
- 2.5 ml onion powder, optional
- kosher salt or sea salt, to taste
- fresh cracked black pepper, to taste
- fresh chopped parsley
- lemon wedges

Preparation

1. For 5 minutes, preheat the Air Fryer to 182°C.
2. The fish fillets should be rinsed then patted dry. Season with garlic powder, lemon pepper, and/or onion powder, salt, and pepper after spraying or coating with olive oil spray. Repeat on the other side.
3. Place perforated air fryer baking paper into the air fryer's base. Spray the paper lightly. (If not using a liner, spray the base of the air fryer basket with enough olive oil spray to keep the fish from sticking.)
4. Position the fish on top of the paper. Place the two lemon slices with the salmon.
5. Air fry the fish at 182°C for 6-12 minutes or until it can be flaked with a fork. Timing will be determined by the thickness of the fillets, the temperature of the fillets, and personal preference.
6. Serve heated with the toasted lemon wedges and sprinkled with minced parsley. If necessary, season with extra seasonings or salt and pepper.

Nutritional information

per servings Calories: 169kcal Carbohydrates: 1g Protein: 34g Fat: 3g Saturated Fat: 1g Cholesterol: 85mg Fiber: 1g Sugar: 1g

109. AIR FRYER KETO FRIED SHRIMP

Prep Time 5 Mins
Cook Time 10 Mins
Total Time 15 Mins
Servings 8

Ingredients

- 25 large shrimp peeled and deveined
- 2/3 cup almond flour
- 3 eggs
- 15 ml ground black pepper
- 5 ml smoked paprika
- 5 ml lemon pepper (optional)

Preparation

1. Preheat your Air Fryer to 198 °C. Use nonstick cooking spray to coat your air fryer basket.
2. Set up two bowls. In one bowl, combine the almond flour, paprika, lemon pepper, and ground black pepper. In the second dish, combine the beaten eggs.
3. Dip the shrimp into the egg mixture, then into the almond flour mixture again. Set aside on a wire rack until all of the shrimp have been used.
4. Cook for 10-12 minutes at 198 °C with the shrimp in a single layer in your preheated air fryer basket. Halfway through, flip the shrimp.
5. Remove from the air fryer until golden brown, and serve immediately.

Nutritional information

per servings Calories: 98kcal Carbohydrates: 1g Protein: 8g Fat: 7g Saturated Fat: 1g Cholesterol: 109mg Fiber: 1g Sugar: 1g

110. AIR FRYER LOBSTER TAILS WITH LEMON-GARLIC BUTTER

Prep: 10 mins
Cook: 10 mins
Total: 20 mins
Servings: 2

Ingredients

- 2 (113 ml) lobster tails
- 56 g butter
- 5 ml lemon zest
- 1 clove garlic, grated
- salt and ground black pepper to taste
- 5 ml chopped fresh parsley
- 2 wedges lemon

Preparation

1. Preheat the air fryer to 195° C.
2. Butterfly lobster tails by cutting kitchen shears lengthwise through the hard upper shells and meat. Cut to, but not through, the shell bottoms. Separate the tail halves. Place the lobster tails in your air fryer basket, flesh side up.
3. Melt the butter in your saucepan over medium heat. Heat the lemon zest and garlic for 30 seconds or until the garlic is fragrant.

4. Brush 28 g of the butter mixture onto the lobster tails; remove any excess smeared butter to avoid contamination with raw lobster. Season the lobster with salt and pepper to taste.
5. Cook until the lobster flesh is opaque, 5 to 7 minutes, in a preheated air fryer.
6. Spoon any remaining butter from the pan over the lobster meat. Serve with lemon wedges and parsley on top.

Nutritional information

per servings calories313; protein 18.1g; carbs 3.3g; fat 25.8g; cholesterol 128.7mg; sodium 590.4mg.

111. AIR FRYER COD

Prep Time 5 mins
Cook Time 16 mins
Total Time 21 mins
Servings 6

Ingredients

- 680 g cod
- 31 g flour regular or gluten-free
- 45 ml plantain flour or use more flour
- 10 ml cajun seasoning or old bay
- 5 ml smoked paprika
- 2.5 ml garlic powder
- 0.6 ml salt
- 5 ml light oil for spraying
- pepper to taste

Preparation

1. Preheat the air fryer basket to 182 °C and spray with oil.
2. In a mixing dish, whisk together the spices and flour.
3. Take the cod out of its box and blot it dry using a paper towel.
4. Each piece of fish should be dipped into the flour spice mixture, then turned over and pressed down to coat completely.
5. Fill the air fryer basket halfway with fish. Make sure there is enough room around each piece of fish for air to circulate.
6. Cook for 6-8 minutes on each side at 182 °C. Cooking time will vary depending on how thick your fish chunks are! Cook for 5 minutes on each side for thinner fillets.
7. Serve hot with lemon.

Nutritional information

per servings Calories: 70kcal Carbohydrates: 15g Protein: 2g Fat: 1g Saturated Fat: 1g Fiber: 1g Sugar: 1g

Prep Time: 10 min
Cook Time: 12 min
Total Time: 22 min
Servings: 4

Ingredients

- 1 (418 g.) can salmon, drained and flaked
- 2 eggs, beaten
- 28 g diced onion
- 14 g chopped fresh parsley

Preparation

1. Preheat your air fryer for 4 mins at 204°C.
2. In a medium mixing dish, combine the salmon, eggs, onion, and parsley. Divide into 8 parties.
3. Place the salmon cakes in a single layer in the air fryer basket and air fry at 204 °C for 6 minutes on each side or until an instant meat thermometer reads 71°C. Continue with the remaining salmon cakes.
4. Garnish with parsley and lemon if desired. Serve and have fun!

Nutrition Information:

per servings Calories: 166 Total Fat: 9gSaturated Fat: 2g Cholesterol: 129mg Sodium: 73mg Carb: 3g Fiber: 1g Sugar: 1g Protein: 16g

Prep Time 5 minutes
Cook Time 10 minutes
Total Time 15 minutes
Servings 2

Ingredients

- 2 6-8 oz tilapia fillets (fresh or frozen)
- 5 ml oil (or air fryer-safe spray)

Preparation

Air Fryer Frozen Tilapia

1. Preheat the air fryer to 204 °C.
2. Oil the air fryer basket or coat the tilapia fillets immediately.
3. Season your fish with the spices of your choice.
4. Place fresh or frozen tilapia fillets in an air fryer basket.
5. Cook frozen tilapia fillets at 204°C for 10-13 minutes, depending on size and thickness. It is advised, but not needed, to flip the pan halfway through the cooking period.

6. Tilapia in an air fryer should be cooked to an internal temperature of at least 63 °C.

Air Fryer Fresh Tilapia

1. Cooking time for fresh tilapia fillets can be reduced by roughly 2-3 minutes.

Nutritional information

per servings Calories: 19kcal Protein: 1g Fat: 2g Saturated Fat: 1g Cholesterol: 1mg

Prep Time: 10 mins
Cook Time: 15 mins
Total Time: 25 mins
Servings; 2

Ingredients

- 2 tilapia filets or other white fish (about 4-6 ounces for each filet)
- 15 ml olive oil or oil spray
- 45 g grated parmesan cheese
- Sea salt, to taste
- black pepper, to taste
- 2.5 ml garlic powder
- 2.5 ml onion powder
- 2.5 ml smoked paprika, or to taste
- fresh chopped parsley, for garnish
- lemon wedges for serving

Preparation

1. Preheat your Air Fryer for 5 mins at 193°C.
2. Set aside the parmesan in a small basin.
3. Drizzle olive oil over the fish liberally or spray with oil spray. Add salt, pepper, garlic powder, onion powder, & paprika to taste. Dip the fish fillets into the cheese mixture, coating both sides. If you want the cheese to adhere to the fish more, dip it in a beaten egg before pushing it into the cheese. The egg will provide additional calories.
4. The perforated parchment paper should be used to line the air fryer basket or tray. Spray the parchment paper lightly with oil spray. Place the coated fish on the parchment paper. Spray the tops of the fish fillets lightly with oil spray.
5. Air fry for 6-12 minutes at 193°C or until the fish can be flaked with a fork. Cooking durations will vary based on the thickness of the fish and the type of air fryer you use.
6. Serve with lemon wedges and chopped parsley on top.

If your air fryer is heated or you are cooking many batches, you may need to shorten the cooking time by a few mins (unless preheating is called for in the recipe).

Nutritional information

per servings Calories: 338kcal, Carbohydrates: 2g, Protein: 44g, Fat: 17g, Saturated Fat: 6g, Fiber: 1g, Sugar: 1g,

115. HONEY DIJON SALMON RECIPE

Prep Time 10 mins
Cook Time 10 mins
Total Time 20 mins
Servings 4

Ingredients

- 4 Skin On Salmon Fillets
- Salt and pepper to taste
- 30 ml Honey
- 30 g Dijon mustard
- 5 ml Garlic powder
- 60 ml Canola oil or olive oil
- 15 ml Parsley flakes
- 60 ml Red Wine Vinegar

Preparation

1. Season the salmon lightly with salt & pepper. Place in a dish or platter.
2. Next, combine the mustard, garlic powder, oil, parsley flakes, and red wine vinegar in a mixing dish.
3. Coat the salmon well with the mixture. Marinate for at least 30 minutes. Then air fry for 10-12 mins at 176°C. Apply the liquid on the salmon halfway through using a pastry brush. Enjoy.

Nutritional information

per servings Calories: 131kcal Carbohydrates: 6g Protein: 21g Fat: 2g Saturated Fat: 1g Cholesterol: 45mg Sodium: 241mg

116. BACON WRAPPED SCALLOPS AIR FRYER RECIPE

Prep Time 5 mins
Cook Time 10 mins
Total Time 15 mins
Servings: 4

Ingredients

- 454 g sea scallops
- 8-9 slices of uncured bacon

Preparation

1. Preheat your air fryer for 5 mins at 187°C.

2. Pat the sea scallops dry with paper towels, then cut the bacon in half lengthwise and wrap a half piece of bacon around each scallop. Rep until all of the scallops have been wrapped with bacon.
3. Cook for 10 minutes, flipping halfway through, or until the scallops are soft and opaque and the bacon is cooked through in the prepared air fryer basket. The scallops should be cooked until they achieve an internal temperature of 54 °C.
4. Serve soon after removing from the basket. Enjoy!

Nutrition Information:

per servings Calories: 246 Fat: 10g Saturated Fat: 3g Cholesterol: 71mg Sodium: 600mg Carbohydrates: 7g Fiber: 0g Sugar: 0g Protein: 32g

117. AIR FRYER SCALLOPS RECIPE

Prep Time 5 mins
Cook Time 6 mins
Total Time 6 mins
Servings: 2

Ingredients

- 454 g sea scallops
- 5 ml lemon pepper seasoning
- Olive oil spray
- Fresh chopped parsley to garnish

Preparation

1. Preheat your air fryer for 5 mins at 204°C.
2. Meanwhile, blot dry the scallops with a paper towel, spray with olive oil, and season on both sides with lemon pepper spice.
3. Cook at 204°C for 6 minutes, flipping halfway through, in the prepared air fryer basket.
4. Remove from your air fryer and top with your preferred sauce.

Nutrition Information:

Calories: 314 Total Fat: 9g Saturated Fat: 1g Cholesterol: 93mg Carbohydrates: 13g Fiber: 0g Sugar: 0g Protein: 47g

118. CRAB LEGS

Prep Time: 5 minutes
Cook Time: 15 minutes
Serving 4

Ingredients

- 57 g salted butter, melted and divided
- 1.3 kg crab legs
- 1.25 ml garlic powder

- Juice of 1/2 medium lemon

Preparation

1. Pour 28 g of butter over the crab legs in a large bowl. Crab legs should be placed in the air fryer basket.
2. The timer should be set for 15 minutes with the temperature adjusted to 204°C.
3. Halfway through the frying process, shake the air fryer basket and throw the crab legs.
4. Combine the remaining butter, garlic powder, and lemon juice in a small bowl.
5. Remove the flesh from the crab legs before serving. With lemon butter, dip.

Nutritional information

per servings Calories: 123 Protein: 15.7 g Fiber: 0.0 g Net Carbohydrates: 0.4 g Fat: 5.6 g Sodium: 756 mg Carbohydrates: 0.4 g Sugar: 0.1 g

119. FRIED TUNA SALAD BITES

Prep Time: 10 mins
Cook Time: 7 mins
servings 12 bites (3 per serving)

Ingredients

- 1 (283 g) can tuna, drained
- 57 g full-fat mayonnaise
- 1 stalk celery, chopped
- 1 medium avocado, peeled, pitted, and mashed
- 96 g blanched finely ground almond flour, divided
- 10 ml coconut oil

Preparation

1. Combine tuna, mayonnaise, celery, and mashed avocado in a big bowl. Create balls out of the mixture.
2. Coconut oil spray is used after rolling balls with almond flour. Put the air fryer basket with the balls inside.
3. Set the temperature to 204°C, then time the cooking for 7 minutes.
4. After five minutes, gently flip the tuna bites. Serve hot.

Nutritional information

per servings calories: 323 protein: 17.3 g fiber: 4.0 g net carbohydrates: 2.3 g fat: 25.4 g sodium: 311 mg Carbohydrates: 6.3 g Sugar: 0.8 g

120. ALMOND PESTO SALMON

Prep Time: 5 mins
Cook Time: 12 mins
serving 2

Ingredients

- 63 g pesto
- 23 g sliced almonds, roughly chopped
- 2 (1 1/2"-thick) salmon fillets (about 113 g each)
- 28 g unsalted butter, melted

Preparation

1. Combine almonds and pesto in a small bowl. Place aside.
2. Fillets should be placed in a 6" circular baking dish.
3. Place half of the pesto mixture on top of each fillet after brushing each one with butter. Put the dish in the basket of the air fryer.
4. The timer should be set for 12 minutes with the temperature adjusted to 198°C.
5. When thoroughly cooked and has attained an internal temperature of at least 63°C, salmon will flake with ease. Serve hot.

Nutritional information

per servings calories: 433 protein: 23.3 g fiber: 2.4 g net carbohydrates: 3.7 g fat: 34.0 g sodium: 341 mg Carbohydrates: 6.1 g Sugar: 0.9 g

SNACKS RECIPE

121. AIR FRYER STEAK BITES RECIPE

Prep Time 5 mins
Cook Time 6 mins
Total Time 11 mins
Servings: 4

Ingredients

- 680 g sirloin steak cut into small cubes
- 5 ml olive oil
- 5 ml Italian seasoning
- Salt and pepper
- 28 g unsalted butter
- 5 ml minced garlic
- Parsley to garnish

Preparation

1. Set aside the steak pieces in a medium bowl with olive oil, Italian seasoning, salt, and pepper to taste.
2. Preheat the air fryer to 204 degrees Celsius for 5 minutes. Once the air fryer is hot, arrange the steak pieces in a single layer in your air fryer basket and air fry at 204 °C for 4-7 minutes or until done to preference.
3. While the steak is cooking, heat the butter and minced garlic until the butter melts and garlic is fragrant.
4. Before serving, toss the air-fried steak bites in the garlic butter with the Parsley.

Nutrition Information:

per servings Calories: 475 Fat: 31g Saturated Fat: 13g Cholesterol: 172mg Sodium: 171mg Carbohydrates: 1g Fiber: 0g Sugar: 0g Protein: 46g

122. AIR FRYER GARLIC PARMESAN WINGS

Prep Time 6 mins
Cook Time 25 mins
Total Time 31 mins
Servings: 3

Ingredients

- 1 kg Chicken Wings
- 4-5 Cloves Garlic minced
- 37 ml Avocado Oil
- 2.5 ml Garlic powder
- 2.5 ml Sea Salt
- 0.6 ml Black Pepper
- 56 g Butter melted
- 22 g Grated Parmesan Cheese
- 2 g Fresh Parsley chopped *optional

Preparation

1. Preheat your air fryer to 200 degrees Celsius. Spray or gently brush the air fryer basket with nonstick cooking spray.
2. Place the wings in a mixing basin. Toss the wings with avocado oil to coat them.
3. Toss the wings with the minced garlic, garlic powder, sea salt, and pepper to coat.
4. Place the wings on the air fryer basket or tray, leaving enough room between them for air to flow (you may need to cook wings in 2 batches depending on basket size).
5. Cook the chicken wings for 25 to 30 minutes, turning halfway through (25 minutes for thawed wings and around 30 minutes for frozen wings, or until done).
6. Toss the cooked wings in a large mixing dish with the melted butter and toss to coat.
7. Toss the wings in the Parmesan cheese and chopped Parsley to coat. Serve.

Nutritional information

per servings Calories: 525kcal Carbohydrates: 3g Protein: 38g Fat: 40g Saturated Fat: 16g Cholesterol: 198mg Sodium: 1500mg Fiber: 1g Sugar: 2g

123. COURGETTE CAKES

Preparation time: 10 minutes
Cooking time: 12 minutes
Servings: 12

Ingredients:

- Cooking spray
- 26 g dill, chopped
- 1 egg
- 60 g whole wheat flour
- Salt and black pepper to the taste
- 1 yellow onion, chopped
- 2 garlic cloves, minced
- 3 Courgette, grated

Preparation

1. In a mixing bowl, combine Courgette, garlic, onion, flour, salt, pepper, egg, and dill; whisk well. Form small patties from this mixture, coat with cooking spray, and cook at 187 °C for 6 minutes on each side.
2. Serve them immediately as a snack.
3. Enjoy!

Nutritional information:

per servings Calories 60, fat 1, fibre 2, carbs 6, protein 2

Preparation time: 10 minutes
Cooking time: 17 minutes
Servings: 6

Ingredients:

- 2.5 ml bicarbonate of soda
- Salt and black pepper to the taste
- 187 g flour
- 1.25 ml basil, dried
- 1 garlic clove, minced
- 28 g basil pesto
- 42 g butter

Preparation

1. Mix salt, pepper, bicarbonate of soda, flour, garlic, cayenne pepper, basil, pesto, and butter in a mixing bowl until a dough forms.
2. Spread this dough on a prepared baking sheet that fits your air fryer, then bake for 17 minutes at 163 °C.
3. Allow cooling before cutting into crackers and serving as a snack.

Nutritional information:

per servings Calories 200, fat 20, fibre 1, carbs 4, protein 7

Preparation time: 10 minutes
Cooking time: 10 minutes
Servings: 4

Ingredients:

- Cooking spray
- 15 radishes, sliced
- Salt and black pepper to the taste
- 53 g chives, chopped

Preparation

1. Arrange radish slices in the basket of your air fryer, spray with cooking oil, season with salt and black pepper to taste, cook at 176°C for 10 minutes, flipping halfway, transfer to bowls, and serve with chives sprinkled on top.

Nutritional information:

per servings Calories 80, fat 1, fibre 1, carbs 1, protein 1

Prep Time 10 minutes
Cook Time 5 minutes
Total Time 15 minutes
Servings 5

Ingredients

- 10 fresh jalapenos
- 170 g cream cheese
- 59 g shredded cheddar cheese
- 2 slices bacon cooked and crumbled
- cooking oil spray

Preparation

1. Cut the jalapenos in half vertically to make two halves per jalapeño.
2. In a moderate mixing bowl, add the cream cheese. To soften, microwave for 15 seconds.
3. Remove the jalapeno's seeds and insides. (If you want spicy poppers, save some of the seeds.)
4. In a mixing dish, combine the cream cheese, crumbled bacon, and shredded cheese. Combine thoroughly.
5. To make more spicy poppers, stir in some of the above-mentioned seeds with the cream cheese mixture.
6. Fill each jalapeño with the cream cheese mixture.
7. Fill the Air Fryer with the poppers. Cooking oil should be sprayed on the poppers.
8. Turn off the Air Fryer. Cook the poppers for 5 to 8 minutes at 187 degrees Celsius.
9. Remove from the Air Fryer and set aside to cool before serving.

Nutritional information

per servings Calories: 61 kcal Carbohydrates: 3g Protein: 3g Fat: 4g

Prep Time: 5 minutes
Cook Time: 5 minutes
Serving: 2

Ingredients

- 1-ounce pork rinds
- 4 ounces shredded cooked chicken
- 1/2 cup shredded Monterey jack cheese
- 1/4 cup sliced pickled jalapeños
- 1/4 cup guacamole
- 1/4 cup full-fat sour cream

Preparation

1. Fill a 6" circular baking pan halfway with pork rinds. Shredded chicken and Monterey jack cheese on top. Insert the pan into the air fryer basket.
2. Set the air fryer temperature to 187°C and the timer for 5 mins, or until the cheese is melted.
3. Serve with jalapenos, guacamole, and sour cream on top.
4. Serve right away.

Nutritional information

per servings calories: 395 protein: 30.1 g fiber: 1.2 g net carbohydrates: 1.8 g fat: 27.5 g sodium: 763 mg Carbohydrates: 3.0 g Sugar: 1.0 g

128. BEEF JERKY

Prep Time: 5 minutes
Cook Time: 4 hours
Servings: 10

Ingredients

- 454 g flat iron beef, thinly sliced
- 60 ml soy sauce (or liquid aminos)
- 10 ml Worcestershire sauce
- 1.25 ml crushed red pepper flakes
- 1.25 ml garlic powder
- 1.25 ml onion powder

Preparation

1. Place all ingredients in a plastic storage bag or covered container and refrigerate for 2 hours.
2. Place each jerky slice in a single layer on the air fryer rack.
3. Set the air fryer temperature to 71°C and the timer for 4 hours.
4. Refrigerate and store in an airtight jar for up to 1 week.

Nutritional information

per servings calories: 85 protein: 10.2 g fiber: 0.0 g net carbohydrates: 0.6 g fat: 3.5 g sodium: 387 mg Carbohydrates: 0.6 g Sugar: 0.2 g

129. PIZZA ROLLS

Prep Time: 15 minutes
Cook Time: 10 minutes
Servings: 24 rolls (3 per serving)

Ingredients

- 224 g shredded mozzarella cheese

- 48 g almond flour
- 2 large eggs
- 72 slices pepperoni
- 8 (28 g) mozzarella string cheese sticks, cut into 3 pieces each
- 28 g unsalted butter, melted
- 1.25 ml garlic powder
- 2.5 ml dried Parsley
- 11 g grated Parmesan cheese

Preparation

1. Place the mozzarella and almond flour in a large microwave-safe mixing bowl. 1 minute in the microwave. Remove the bowl and continue to mix until a ball of dough forms. If necessary, microwave for another 30 seconds.
2. Crack the eggs into the mixing basin and stir until smooth dough ball forms. Wet your hands and knead the dough for a few seconds.
3. Cut two big sheets of parchment paper and coat one side with nonstick cooking spray. Place the dough ball between the two sheets and spray sides up. Roll out the dough to 1/4" thickness with a rolling pin.
4. Cut the pie into 24 rectangles using a knife. Place 3 pepperoni slices and 1 piece of string cheese on each rectangle.
5. Cover the pepperoni and cheese mixture by folding the rectangle in half. Pinch or roll the sides shut. Cut a piece of parchment paper to suit your air fryer basket and set it inside. Place the rolls on the parchment paper.
6. Set the air fryer temperature to 176°C and the timer for 10 minutes.
7. After 5 minutes, remove the pizza rolls from the fryer and turn them. Restart the frying and cook until the pizza rolls are golden.
8. Combine the butter, garlic powder, and Parsley in a small bowl. Brush the mixture over the baked pizza rolls and top with Parmesan. Serve hot.

Nutritional information

per servings calories: 333 protein: 20.7 g fiber: 0.8 g net carbohydrates: 2.5 g fat: 24.0 g sodium: 708 mg Carbohydrates: 3.3 g Sugar: 0.9 g

130. SMOKY BBQ ROASTED ALMONDS

Prep Time: 5 minutes
Cook Time: 6 minutes
Servings: 4 (1/4 cup per serving)

Ingredients

- 143 g raw almonds

- 10 ml coconut oil
- 5 ml chilli powder
- 1.25 ml cumin
- 1.25 ml smoked paprika
- 1.25 ml onion powder

Preparation

1. Toss all ingredients in a large mixing basin until almonds are equally covered with oil and spices. Fill the air fryer basket halfway with almonds.
2. Set the air fryer temperature to 160°C and the timer for 6 minutes.
3. Halfway through the cooking time, toss the fryer basket. Allow it to cool totally.

Nutritional information

per servings calories 182 protein: 6.2 g fibre: 3.3 g net carbohydrates: 3.3 g fat: 16.3 g sodium: 19 mg Carbohydrates: 6.6 g Sugar: 1.1 g

131. BACON-WRAPPED BRIE

Prep Time: 5 minutes
Cook Time: 10 minutes
Servings: 8

Ingredients

- 4 slices sugar-free bacon
- 1 (227 g) round Brie

Preparation

1. Form an X with two pieces of bacon. Place the third piece of bacon across the middle of the X. Place the fourth piece of bacon across the X vertically. It should resemble a plus symbol (+) above an X. Put the Brie in the middle of the bacon.
2. Wrap the bacon around the Brie and secure it with toothpicks. Place the bacon-wrapped Brie on top of a piece of parchment cut to fit your air fryer basket. Place the air fryer basket inside.
3. Set the air fryer temperature to 204°C and the timer for 10 minutes.
4. When 3 minutes have passed, carefully flipBrie.
5. When finished, the bacon will be crisp, and the cheese will be soft and melty. Cut into eight pieces to serve.

Nutritional information

per servings Calories: 116 protein: 7.7 g fiber: 0.0 g net carbohydrates: 0.2 g fat: 8.9 g sodium: 259 mg carbohydrates: 0.2 g sugar: 0.1 g

132. MOZZARELLA STICKS

Prep Time: 1 hour
Cook Time: 10 minutes
Servings: 12 sticks (3 per serving)

Ingredients

- 6 (28 g) mozzarella string cheese sticks
- 45 g grated Parmesan cheese
- 14 g pork rinds, finely ground
- 5 ml dried Parsley
- 2 large eggs

Preparation

1. Cut the mozzarella sticks in half on a chopping board. Freeze for 45 minutes or until the mixture is stiff. If freezing overnight, remove frozen sticks after 1 hour and store them in an airtight zip-top storage bag before re-freezing.
2. Combine the Parmesan, ground pork rinds, and Parsley in a large mixing basin.
3. Whisk the eggs in a medium mixing basin.
4. To coat, dip a frozen mozzarella stick into beaten eggs and then into the Parmesan mixture. Repeat with the remaining sticks. Fill your air fryer basket with mozzarella sticks.
5. Preheat the air fryer to 204°C and set the timer for 10 minutes or until brown.
6. Serve hot.

Nutritional information

per servings calories: 236 protein: 19.2 g fiber: 0.0 g net carbohydrates: 4.7 g fat: 13.8 g sodium: 609 mg Carbohydrates: 4.7 g Sugar: 1.1 g

133. PORK RIND TORTILLAS

Prep Time: 10 minutes
Cook Time: 5 minutes
Servings: 4 tortillas (1 per serving)

Ingredients

- 28 g pork rinds
- 62 g shredded mozzarella cheese
- 30 ml full-fat cream cheese
- 1 large egg

Preparation

1. Pulse the pork rinds in your food processor until coarsely ground.
2. Fill a large heat-proof dish halfway with mozzarella. Add the cream cheese in tiny pieces to the mixing bowl. Microwave for 30 seconds or until both pieces

of cheese are melted and readily combined into a ball. To the cheese mixture, add the crushed pork rinds and the egg.

3. Continue to whisk the ingredients until it forms a ball. If it cools too quickly and the cheese hardens, microwave for 10 seconds more.

4. Make four little balls out of the dough. Roll each dough ball between two pieces of parchment paper into a 1/4" flat layer.

5. Place the tortillas in a single layer in the air fryer basket, working in batches if required.

6. Set the air fryer temperature to 204°C and the timer for 5 minutes.

7. When fully cooked, the tortillas will be crispy and firm.

8. Serve right away.

Nutritional information

per servings Calories: 145 protein: 10.7 g fiber: 0.0 g net carbohydrates: 0.8 g fat: 10.0 g sodium: 291 mg carbohydrates: 0.8 g sugar: 0.5 g

134. BACON JALAPEÑO CHEESE BREAD

Prep Time: 10 minutes
Cook Time: 15 minutes
Serving: 8 sticks (2 sticks per serving)

Ingredients

- 450 g shredded mozzarella cheese
- 22 g grated Parmesan cheese
- 104 g chopped pickled jalapeños
- 2 large eggs
- 4 slices sugar-free bacon, cooked and chopped

Preparation

1. In a large bowl, combine each item. To fit your air fryer basket, cut a piece of parchment.

2. Apply a little water to your hands and spread the mixture into a circle. The size of your fryer may need you to divide this into two smaller pieces of cheese bread.

3. Put the cheese bread and parchment paper in the air fryer basket.

4. Set the timer for 15 minutes and raise the temperature to 160°C.

5. After 5 minutes, carefully turn the bread.

6. The top will be golden brown when the food is done cooking.

7. Serve hot.

Nutritional information

per serving calories: 273 protein: 20.1 g fiber: 0.1 g net carbohydrates: 2.1 g fat: 18.1 g sodium: 749 mg
Carbohydrates: 2.3 g Sugar: 0.7 g

135. MOZZARELLA PIZZA CRUST

Prep Time: 5 minutes
Cook Time: 10 minutes
Serving: 1

Ingredients

- 120 ml shredded whole-milk mozzarella cheese
- 30 ml blanched finely ground almond flour
- 15 ml full-fat cream cheese
- 1 large egg white

Preparation

1. Mix the cream cheese, mozzarella, and almond flour in a medium microwave-safe bowl. 30 seconds in the microwave. Stir until a dough ball forms that is smooth. Stir in the egg white until a soft, spherical dough forms.

2. Press into a 6" round pizza crust.

3. Place the crust on paper that has been cut to fit your air fryer basket. Place in the air fryer basket.

4. Set the timer for 10 minutes and raise the temperature to 176°C.

5. After five minutes, flip the crust, and then top with any desired toppings. Cooking should continue until golden. Serve right away.

Nutritional information

per serving calories: 314protein: 19.9 g fiber: 1.5 g net carbohydrates: 3.6 g fat: 22.7 g sodium: 457 mg
Carbohydrates: 5.1 g Sugar: 1.8 g

DESSERTS RECIPE

136. PUMPKIN COOKIE WITH CREAM CHEESE FROSTING

Prep Time: 10 mins
Cook Time: 7 mins
Servings: 6

Ingredients

- 48 g blanched finely ground almond flour
- 96 g powdered erythritol divided
- 28 g butter, softened
- 1 large egg
- 2.5 ml unflavored gelatin
- 2.5 ml bicarbonate of soda
- 2.5 ml vanilla extract
- 2.5 ml pumpkin pie spice
- 30 g pure pumpkin purée
- 2.5 ml ground cinnamon divided
- 40 g low-carb, sugar-free chocolate chips
- 85 g full-fat cream cheese, softened

Preparation

1. In a large mixing bowl, combine almond flour and 50 g erythritol. In a mixing basin, combine the butter, egg, and gelatin.
2. After mixing in the bicarbonate of soda, vanilla, pumpkin pie spice, pumpkin purée, and 1.25 mL cinnamon, fold in the chocolate chips.
3. Fill a 6-inch circular baking pan halfway with the batter. Place the pan inside the air fryer basket.
4. Set the air fryer to 148°C and set the timer to 7 minutes.
5. The top should be golden brown when done, and a toothpick inserted into the centre should come out clean. Allow at least 20 minutes for cooling.
6. Combine cream cheese, the remaining 1.25 ml cinnamon, and the remaining 96 g erythritol in a large mixing bowl. Using an electric mixer, whip until foamy. Spread the cooled cookie with the mixture. Garnish with more cinnamon if desired.

Nutritional information

per servings Calories: 199 Protein: 4.8 g fibre: 1.9 g net carbohydrates: 2.9 g sugar alcohol: 16.7 g fat: 16.2 g sodium: 105 mg Carbohydrates: 21.5 g Sugar: 1.1 g

137. MINI CHEESECAKE

Prep Time: 10 mins
Cook Time: 15 mins
Servings: 2

Ingredients

- 50 g walnuts
- 28 g salted butter
- 30 ml granular erythritol
- 4 ounces full-fat cream cheese, softened
- 1 large egg
- 2.5 ml vanilla extract
- 30 ml powdered erythritol

Preparation

1. Combine walnuts, butter, and granular erythritol in a food processor. Pulse the items together until a dough forms.
2. Place the dough in the air fryer basket in a 4" springform pan.
3. Set the air fryer to 204°C and the timer to 5 minutes.
4. When the timer goes off, remove the crust and lay it away to cool.
5. In a medium mixing bowl, blend the cream cheese, egg, vanilla extract, and powdered erythritol until smooth.
6. Spoon the mixture on top of the fried walnut crust and place your air fryer basket in the air fryer
7. Set the air fryer to 148°C and the timer to 10 minutes.
8. Refrigerate for at least two hrs before serving.

Nutritional information

per servings Calories: 531 Protein: 11.4 g fibre: 2.3 g net carbohydrates: 5.1 g sugar alcohol: 24.0 g fat: 48.3 g sodium: 333 mg Carbohydrates: 31.4 g Sugar: 2.9 g

138. PUMPKIN SPICE PECANS

Prep Time: 5 mins
Cook Time: 6 mins
Servings: 4

Ingredients

- 125 g whole pecans
- 60 ml granular erythritol
- 1 large egg white
- 2.5 ml ground cinnamon
- 2.5 ml pumpkin pie spice
- 2.5 ml vanilla extract

Preparation

1. Combine all of the ingredients in a large mixing bowl and toss until the pecans are uniformly coated. In the air fryer, place the air fryer basket.
2. Set the temperature to 148°C and the timer for 6 minutes.
3. While cooking, toss twice or three times.
4. Allow cooling completely. For up to three days, store in an airtight container.

Nutritional information

per servings Calories: 178 protein: 3.2 g fiber: 2.6 g net carbohydrates: 1.4 g sugar alcohol: 15.0 g fat: 17.0 g sodium: 13 mg carbohydrates: 19.0 g sugar: 1.1 g

139. ALMOND BUTTER COOKIE BALLS

Prep Time: 5 minutes
Cook Time: 10 minutes
Servings: 10 balls (1 ball per serving)

Ingredients

- 256 g almond butter
- 1 large egg
- 5 ml vanilla extract
- 38 g low-carb protein powder
- 5 g powdered erythritol
- 18 g shredded unsweetened coconut
- 40 g low-carb, sugar-free chocolate chips
- 2.5 ml ground cassia

Preparation

1. In a large mixing bowl, combine almond butter and egg. Combine the vanilla extract, protein powder, and erythritol in a mixing bowl.
2. In a mixing dish, combine the coconut, chocolate chips, and cassia. Fill 6 cups halfway with balls. "Place the spherical baking pan in the air fryer basket.
3. Set the air fryer to 160°C and the timer to 10 minutes.
4. Allow to cool completely. Refrigerate for up to 4 days in an airtight container.

Nutritional information

per servings Calories: 224 protein: 11.2 g fiber: 3.6 g net carbohydrates: 1.3 g sugar alcohol: 10.0 g fat: 16.0 g sodium: 40 mg carbohydrates: 14.9 g sugar: 1.3 g

140. PECAN BROWNIES

Prep Time: 10 minutes
Cook Time: 20 minutes

Servings: 6

Ingredients

- 48 g blanched finely ground almond flour
- 118 ml powdered erythritol
- 30 ml unsweetened cocoa powder
- 2.5 ml bicarbonate of soda
- 57 g unsalted butter, softened
- 1 large egg
- 30 g chopped pecans
- 40 g low-carb, sugar-free chocolate chips

Preparation

1. In a large mixing bowl, combine almond flour, erythritol, cocoa powder, and bicarbonate of soda. Incorporate the butter and egg.
2. Combine the pecans and chocolate chips in a mixing bowl. Fill a 6-inch circular baking pan halfway with the mixture. Place the pan inside the air fryer basket.
3. Set the air fryer to 148°C and the timer to 20 minutes.
4. When properly cooked, a toothpick inserted into the centre will come out clean. Allow the mixture to cool and firm up for 20 minutes.

Nutritional information

per servings Calories: 215 Protein: 4.2 g fibre: 2.8 g net carbohydrates: 2.3 g sugar alcohol: 16.7 g fat: 18.9 g sodium: 53 mg Carbohydrates: 21.8 g Sugar: 0.6 g

141. CHOCOLATE ESPRESSO MINI CHEESECAKE

Prep Time: 5 minutes
Cook Time: 15 minutes
Servings: 2

Ingredients

- 50 g walnuts
- 28 g salted butter
- 30 ml granular erythritol
- 113 g full-fat cream cheese, softened
- 1 large egg
- 2.5 ml vanilla extract
- 30 ml powdered erythritol
- 10 ml unsweetened cocoa powder
- 5 ml espresso powder

Preparation

1. In a food processor, combine walnuts, butter, and granular erythritol. Pulse until the ingredients are combined and a dough forms.
2. Place the dough in the air fryer basket after pressing it onto a 4" springform pan.

3. Set the air fryer temperature to 204°C and the timer for 5 minutes.
4. When the timer goes off, remove the crust and set it aside to cool.
5. Cream cheese, egg, vanilla extract, powdered erythritol, cocoa powder, and espresso powder should be combined in a medium mixing dish until smooth.
6. Place the air fryer basket in the air fryer basket and spoon the mixture on top of the fried walnut crust.
7. Set the temperature to 148° C and the timer to 10 minutes.
8. Refrigerate for 2 hours before serving.

Nutritional information

per servings Calories: 535 Protein: 11.6 g fibre: 7.2 g net carbohydrates: 5.9 g sugar alcohol: 24.0 g fat: 48.4 g sodium: 336 mg Carbohydrates: 37.1 g Sugar: 5.9 g

142. COCONUT FLOUR MUG CAKE

Prep Time: 5 minutes
Cook Time: 25 minutes
Servings: 1

Ingredients

- 1 large egg
- 14 g coconut flour
- 30 g double cream
- 30 ml granular erythritol
- 1.25 ml vanilla extract
- 1.25 ml bicarbonate of soda

Preparation

1. In a 4" ramekin, whisk the egg, then add the remaining ingredients. Stir until well combined. In the air fryer, place the air fryer basket.
2. Set the air fryer to 148°C and the timer to 25 minutes. A toothpick should come out clean after you're finished. Serve straight from the ramekin with a spoon. Serve immediately.

Nutritional information

per servings Calories: 237 Protein: 9.9 g fibre: 5.0 g net carbohydrates: 5.7 g sugar alcohol: 30.0 g fat: 16.4 g sodium: 213 mg Carbohydrates: 40.7 g Sugar: 4.2 g

143. TOASTED COCONUT FLAKES

Prep Time: 5 mins
Cook Time: 3 mins
Servings: 4

Ingredients

- 93 g unsweetened coconut flakes
- 10 ml coconut oil
- 60 ml granular erythritol
- 0.6 ml salt

Preparation

1. Toss the coconut flakes with the oil in a large mixing bowl until evenly coated. Season with salt and erythritol.
2. Fill half of the air fryer basket with coconut flakes.
3. Set the air fryer to 148°C and the timer to 3 minutes.
4. After one minute, throw the flakes. Cook for an additional minute if you want a more golden coconut flake.
5. For up to three days, store in an airtight container.

Nutritional information

per servings Calories: 165 protein: 1.3 g fiber: 2.7 g net carbohydrates: 2.6 g sugar alcohol: 15.0 g fat: 15.5 g sodium: 76 mg carbohydrates: 20.3 g sugar: 0.5 g

144. VANILLA POUND CAKE

Prep Time: 10 mins
Cook Time: 25 mins
Servings: 6

Ingredients

- 96 g blanched finely ground almond flour
- 56 g salted butter, melted
- 120 ml granular erythritol
- 5 ml vanilla extract
- 5 ml bicarbonate of soda
- 123 g full-fat sour cream
- 28 g full-fat cream cheese, softened
- 2 large eggs

Preparation

1. In a large mixing bowl, combine almond flour, butter, and erythritol.
2. Blend in the vanilla extract, bicarbonate of soda, sour cream, and cream cheese until smooth. Incorporate the eggs.
3. Fill a 6-inch round baking pan halfway with the batter and place it in the air fryer basket.
4. Set the air fryer to 148°C and the timer to 25 minutes.
5. When the cake is ready, a toothpick inserted into the centre should come out clean; the centre should not be moist; allow it to cool completely before transferring it; otherwise, the cake may crumble.

Nutritional information

per servings Calories: 253 protein: 6.9 g fiber: 2.0 g net carbohydrates: 3.2 g sugar alcohol: 20.0 g fat: 22.6 g sodium: 191 mg carbohydrates: 25.2 g sugar: 1.5 g

145. RASPBERRY DANISH BITES

Prep Time: 30 mins
Cook Time: 7 mins
Servings: 10

Ingredients

- 96 g blanched finely ground almond flour
- 5 ml bicarbonate of soda
- 45 ml granular Swerve
- 56 g full-fat cream cheese, softened
- 1 large egg
- 170 g sugar-free raspberry preserves

Preparation

1. Combine all ingredients except the preserves in a large mixing bowl until a moist dough forms.
2. Place the bowl in the freezer for 20 minutes or until the dough is cool enough to flatten into a ball.
3. Roll the dough into ten balls, then gently press each one in the centre. Place 17 g preserves in the centre of each ball.
4. Fit your air fryer basket with parchment paper.
5. Place each Danish bite on the parchment paper, flattening the bottom carefully.
6. Set the air fryer to 204°C and the timer to 7 minutes.
7. Allow to cool completely before transferring to avoid collapse.

Nutritional information

per servings Calories: 96 Protein: 3.4 g fibre: 1.3 g net carbohydrates: 4.0 g sugar alcohol: 4.5 g fat: 7.7 g sodium: 76 mg Carbohydrates: 9.8 g Sugar: 2.4 g

146. CREAM CHEESE DANISH

Prep Time: 20 minutes
Cook Time: 15 minutes
Serving: 6

Ingredients

- 72 g blanched finely ground almond flour
- 113 g shredded mozzarella cheese
- 142 g full-fat cream cheese divided
- 2 large egg yolks
- 18 g powdered erythritol divided
- 10 ml vanilla extract divided

Preparation

1. Add 28 g of cream cheese, mozzarella, and almond flour to a sizable microwave-safe bowl. After combining, microwave for one minute.
2. Add egg yolks to the bowl after stirring. Stir consistently until soft dough forms. Add 12 g erythritol and 5 ml vanilla to the dough.
3. To fit your air fryer basket, cut a piece of parchment. Warm water-wet hands are used to flatten the dough into a 14"-thick rectangle.
4. Mix the remaining cream cheese, erythritol, and vanilla in a medium bowl. Put this cream cheese mixture on the dough rectangle's right side. The dough is folded over and sealed by pressing the left side. Place it in your air fryer basket.

5. The timer should be set for 15 minutes with the temperature adjusted to 165°C.
6. Turn the Danish over after seven minutes.
7. Remove the Danish from the parchment when the timer goes off, and let it cool entirely before slicing.

Nutritional information

per serving calories: 185 protein: 7.4 g fibre: 0.5 g net carbohydrates: 2.3 g sugar alcohol: 18.0 g fat: 14.5 g sodium: 205 mg Carbohydrates: 20.8 g Sugar: 1.3 g

147. CARAMEL MONKEY BREAD

Prep Time: 15 minutes
Cook Time: 12 minutes
Servings: 6 (2 pieces per serving)

Ingredients

- 48 g blanched finely ground almond flour
- 120 ml low-carb vanilla protein powder
- 18 g granular erythritol, divided
- 2.5 ml bicarbonate of soda
- 113 g salted butter, melted and divided
- 28 g full-fat cream cheese, softened
- 1 large egg
- 60 ml double cream
- 2.5 ml vanilla extract

Preparation

1. Almond flour, protein powder, 12 g erythritol, bicarbonate of soda, 75 g butter, cream cheese, and egg should all be combined in a sizable basin. You'll get a soft, sticky dough.
2. For 20 mins, place the dough in the freezer. It will have sufficient firmness to roll into balls. Roll into twelve balls after wetting your hands with warm water. Into a 6" round baking dish, put the balls.
3. Melt the remaining butter and the remaining erythritol in a medium skillet over medium heat. Add cream and vanilla after turning the heat to low and continuing to whisk the mixture until it turns brown. Remove from heat and whisk continuously while letting it thicken for a few minutes.
4. Put the baking dish into the air fryer basket while the mixture cools.
5. The timer should be set for 6 minutes with the temperature adjusted to 160°C.
6. Flip the monkey bread over onto a platter and place it back into the baking pan when the timer beeps. Cook for a further 4 minutes or until the tops are fully browned.
7. After adding the caramel sauce, let the monkey bread bake for two more minutes. Allow cooling before serving.

Nutritional information

per serving calories: 322 protein: 20.4 g fibre: 1.7 g net carbohydrates: 2.0 g sugar alcohol: 30.0 g fat: 24.5 g sodium: 301 mg Carbohydrates: 33.7 g Sugar: 0.9 g

148. PAN PEANUT BUTTER COOKIES

Prep Time: 5 minutes
Cook Time: 8 minutes
Serving: 8

Ingredients

- 250 g no-sugar-added smooth peanut butter
- 8 g granular erythritol
- 1 large egg
- 5 ml vanilla extract

Preparation

1. Blend all the ingredients in a large basin. The liquid will start to thicken after two more minutes of stirring.
2. Eight disks of the mixture should be formed by rolling it into balls and gently pressing down.
3. To fit your air fryer, cut a piece of parchment to size and put it in the basket. Working in batches as needed, arranging the cookies on the parchment.
4. The timer should be set for 8 minutes with the temperature adjusted to 160°C.
5. At the six-minute point, turn the cookies. Serve after having fully cooled.

Nutritional information

per serving calories: 210 protein: 8.8 g fibre: 2.0 g net carbohydrates: 2.1 g sugar alcohol: 10.0 g fat: 17.5 g sodium: 8 mg Carbohydrates: 14.1 g Sugar: 1.1 g

149. PROTEIN POWDER DOUGHNUT HOLES

Prep Time: 25 mins
Cook Time: 6 mins
serving: 12 holes (2 per serving)

Ingredients

- 48 g blanched finely ground almond flour
- 120 ml low-carb vanilla protein powder
- 12 g granular erythritol
- 2.5 ml bicarbonate of soda
- 1 large egg
- 71 g unsalted butter, melted
- 2.5 ml vanilla extract

Preparation

1. In a sizable bowl, combine each item. Place for 20 minutes in the freezer.
2. Roll the dough into twelve balls after wetting your hands with water.
3. To fit your air fryer basket, cut a piece of parchment. Doughnut holes should be put into the air fryer basket on top of parchment paper in batches as necessary.
4. The timer should be set for 6 minutes with the temperature adjusted to 193°C.
5. Halfway through cooking, turn the doughnut holes.
6. Allow cooling before serving.

Nutritional information

per serving calories: 221 protein: 19.8 g fibre: 1.7 g net carbohydrates: 1.5 g sugar alcohol: 20.0 g fat: 14.3 g sodium: 160 mg Carbohydrates: 23.2 g Sugar: 0.4 g

150. LAYERED PEANUT BUTTER CHEESECAKE BROWNIES

Prep Time: 20 minutes
Cook Time: 35 minutes
Serving: 6

Ingredients

- 48 g blanched finely ground almond flour
- 204 g powdered erythritol divided
- 30 ml unsweetened cocoa powder
- 2.5 ml bicarbonate of soda
- 57 g unsalted butter, softened
- 2 large eggs, divided
- 227 g full-fat cream cheese, softened
- 60 ml double cream
- 5 ml vanilla extract
- 32 g no-sugar-added peanut butter

Preparation

1. Almond flour, 102 g erythritol, cocoa powder, and bicarbonate of soda should all be combined in a sizable basin. Add butter and one egg, and stir.
2. Into a 6" round baking pan, scoop the mixture. In the air fryer basket, put the pan.
3. Set the timer for 20 minutes and raise the temperature to 149°C.
4. A toothpick inserted in the middle will come out clean when the food is thoroughly cooked. Give the food 20 minutes to completely cool and set.
5. Cream cheese, the remaining 102 g of erythritol, double cream, vanilla, peanut butter, and the last egg should be beaten until frothy in a large bowl.
6. Mixture over brownies that have cooled. Reposition the pan into the air fryer basket.
7. Set the timer for 15 minutes and raise the temperature to 149°C.
8. When finished, the cheesecake should be mainly firm, slightly jiggling, and slightly browned. Afterwards, chill for two hours before serving.

Nutritional information

per serving calories: 347 protein: 8.3 g fibre: 2.0 g net carbohydrates: 3.8 g sugar alcohol: 24.0 g fat: 30.9 g sodium: 207 mg Carbohydrates: 29.8 g Sugar: 2.2 g

CONCLUSION

Air fryers are now one of the most innovative kitchen gadgets and one of the most widely utilized cooking techniques.

An air fryer allows you to rapidly cook great, healthy meals! Cooking delicious meals for yourself and your family does not need becoming a master chef!

You only need an air fryer and this a wonderful low crab air fryer cookbook to get started.

You'll prepare the best dishes ever in no time, and your handmade meals will impress everyone around you!

Believe in us! Begin your new culinary adventure by purchasing an air fryer and this collection of useful air fryer recipes.

30-DAY MEAL PLAN

Day	Breakfast	Lunch	Dinner	Desserts/Snacks
1	Quick And Easy Bacon Strips	Spaghetti Squash Alfredo	Air Fryer Scallops Recipe	Layered Peanut Butter
2	Scrambled Eggs	Air Fryer Green Beans	Courgette Cauliflower Fritters	Pesto Crackers
3	Air Fryer Sausage Patties	Cheesy Zoodle Bake	Bacon Wrapped Scallops Air Fryer Recipe	Air Fryer Garlic Parmesan Wings
4	Egg Muffins	Keto Meatballs With Almond Flour	Air Fryer Healthy White Fish With Garlic & Lemon	Bacon-Wrapped Brie
5	Banana Nut Cake	Whole Roasted Lemon Cauliflower	Prosciutto-Wrapped Parmesan Asparagus	Cheesecake Brownies
6	Pumpkin Spice Muffins	Crispy Beef And Broccoli Stir-Fry	Classic Mini Meatloaf	Courgette Cakes
7	Cheesy Cauliflower Hash Browns	Keto Bacon Cheddar Stuffed Air Fryer Burgers	Fried Tuna Salad Bites	Mozzarella Sticks
8	Bacon, Egg, And Cheese Roll-Ups	Bacon-Wrapped Hot Dog	Air Fryer Cheesy Bacon Hasselback Chicken	Smoky Bbq Roasted Almonds

9	Pancake Cake	Crispy Pork Chop Salad	Air Fryer Mahi Mahi Recipe	Bacon Jalapeño Cheese Bread
10	Veggie Frittata	Best Air Fryer Turkey Breast Recipe	Crab Legs	Air Fryer Steak Bites Recipe
11	Lemon Poppy Seed Cake	Low Carb Keto Paleo Baked Chicken Nuggets In The Air Fryer	Crusted White Fish (Keto)	Pizza Rolls
12	Sausage And Cheese Balls	Almond Pesto Salmon	Air Fryer Lemon Pepper Wings	Mozzarella Pizza Crust
13	Cheesy Bell Pepper Eggs	Honey Dijon Salmon Recipe	Easy Air Fryer Chicken Thighs Bone-In, Skin-On	Beef Jerky
14	Spaghetti Squash Fritters	Best Air Fryer Chicken Fajitas Recipe	Spicy Spinach Artichoke Dip	Pork Rind Nachos
15	Breakfast Calzone	Bacon-Wrapped Onion Rings	Chicken Pizza Crust	Pumpkin Cookie With Cream Cheese Frosting
16	Easy Air Fryer Jalapeno Poppers	Air Fryer Cod	Air Fryer Corned Beef	Mini Cheesecake
17	Pan Peanut Butter Cookies	Veggie Quesadilla	Mozzarella-Stuffed Meatball	Pumpkin Spice Pecans
18	Crispy Brussels Sprouts	Garlic Herb Butter Roasted Radishes	Chorizo And Beef Burger	Holes
19	Kale Chips	Air Fryer Lobster Tails With	Air Fryer Chicken Drumsticks	Raspberry Danish Bites

		Lemon-Garlic Butter		
20	Roasted Veggie Bowl	Peppercorn-Crusted Beef Tenderloin	Air Fryer Keto Fried Shrimp	Coconut Flour Mug Cake
21	Quiche-Stuffed Peppers	Air Fryer London Broil	Air Fryer Asparagus	Chocolate Espresso Mini Cheesecake
22	Buffalo Cauliflower	Air Fryer Shrimp Recipe	Cheesy Cauliflower Pizza Crust	Vanilla Pound Cake
23	Air Fryer Frozen Okra	Garlic Parmesan Chicken Wings	Perfect Air Fryer Ribeye Steak Recipe	Crispy Radish Chips
24	Avocado Fries	Greek Stuffed Aubergine	Air Fryer Chicken Wings	Pecan Brownies
25	Broccoli Crust Pizza	Air Fryer Sausage Patties	Air Fryer Marinated Flank Steak	Almond Butter Cookie Balls
26	Air Fryer Turnip Fries	Air Fryer Tilapia (Frozen Or Fresh)	Air Fryer French Onion Chicken Breast And Fontina Cheese	Toasted Coconut Flakes
27	Egg Muffins	Air Fryer Pork Chops And Garlic Broccoli	Lamb Shanks And Carrots	Protein Powder Doughnut
28	Quick And Easy Bacon Strips	Greek Lamb Pita Pockets	Cornish Hen In Air Fryer (Super Easy)	Cream Cheese Danish
29	Banana Nut Cake	Air Fryer Frozen Chicken Breast	Caprese Aubergine Stacks	Pork Rind Tortillas
30	Roasted Broccoli Salad Broccoli	Easy Air Fryer Salmon Cakes Recipe	Pecan Crusted Chicken | Low Carb Pecan Chicken Recipe	Caramel Monkey Bread

COOKING TIMES

OVEN	AIR FRYER
1O MINUTES	8 MINUTES
15 MINUTES	12 MINUTES
20 MINUTES	16 MINUTES
25 MINUTES	20 MINUTES
30 MINUTES	24 MINUTES
35 MINUTES	28 MINUTES
40 MINUTES	32 MINUTES
45 MINUTES	36 MINUTES
50 MINUTES	40 MINUTES
55 MINUTES	44 MINUTES
1 HOUR	48 MINUTES

AIR FRYER CONVERSION CHART

OVEN	OVEN FAN	AIR FRYER
190 ℃	170 ℃	150 ℃
200 ℃	180 ℃	160 ℃
210 ℃	190 ℃	170 ℃
220 ℃	200 ℃	180 ℃
230 ℃	210 ℃	190 ℃

COST OF COOKING CHART

APPLIANCE	COST PER DAY	COST PER WEEK	COST PER MONTH	COST PER YEAR
ELECTRIC COOKER	87P	£6.09	£26.38	£316.54
DUAL FUEL COOKER (GAS AND ELECTRIC)	72P	£5.08	£22.00	£264.03
GAS COOKER	33P	£2.23	£10.07	£120.83
SLOW COOKER	16P	£1.15	£4.98	£59.76
AIR FRYER	**14P**	**£1.01**	**£4.40**	**£52.74**
MICROWAVE	8P	58 P	£2.50	£30.02

ALPHABETICAL RECIPE INDEX